Forum Sprache
**English
Grammar Exercises**

Hans G. Hoffmann · Friedhold Schmidt

English Grammar Exercises
Arbeitsbuch
Grammatik · Sprachgebrauch für Fortgeschrittene

Max Hueber Verlag

Das Werk und seine Teile sind urheberrechtlich geschützt.
Jede Verwertung in anderen als den gesetzlich zugelassenen
Fällen bedarf deshalb der vorherigen schriftlichen
Einwilligung des Verlages.

| 7. 6. 5. | Die letzten Ziffern |
| 2005 04 03 02 01 | bezeichnen Zahl und Jahr des Druckes. |

Alle Drucke dieser Auflage können, da unverändert,
nebeneinander benutzt werden.
4. unveränderte Auflage 1985
© 1985 Max Hueber Verlag, D-85737 Ismaning
Umschlaggestaltung: Werbeagentur Braun & Voigt, Heidelberg
Satz: J. Ebner, Ulm
Druck: Ludwig Auer GmbH, Donauwörth
Printed in Germany
ISBN 3–19–002158–9

Preface

This collection of grammar exercises is intended for advanced English language courses at universities, teacher-training colleges, and language schools. The students attending such courses will have had up to nine years of English at school and in many cases may have spent up to twelve months in an English-speaking country. With a language background such as this, the students should be in a position to study the more involved aspects of present-day English usage and at the same time to gain an insight into the structural peculiarities of modern English.

With the needs of these students in mind, the authors have concentrated entirely on those areas of usage where even the advanced learner frequently goes astray, either because of the inherent difficulty and complexity of the syntactic structures involved or because of intralingual or interlingual interference.

The exercises in this volume are mainly of the fill-in and translation type. This may surprise teachers and students familiar with the wide variety of stimulus-response type situational drills now common at the elementary and intermediate levels of language teaching. The reason for the prominence of fill-in and translation exercises in this book is, of course, that the rigid parallelism of language-laboratory type drills would be completely out of place at the level of competence for which this material is intended.

The English practice sentences included are mostly authentic, i.e., they were taken from contemporary British and American novels, newspapers, magazines, and plays. It follows that this material should be fairly representative of the actual usage of educated native speakers in Britain and America.

It is hoped that the organization and layout of the subject matter makes the book equally suitable for systematic course work, sporadic remedial exercises, and reference purposes.

It goes without saying that a practice book of this nature cannot be a substitute for a comprehensive reference grammar. Students would therefore do well to use these exercises in conjunction with a systematic grammar such as *Grammatik der englischen Sprache* by Adolf Lamprecht (new edition 1970 published by Cornelsen, Berlin).

The authors are indebted to Mrs Hilary Heltay and Mr Kenneth Dixon for reading the manuscript and the proofs and offering many valuable suggestions for improvement. In fairness it should be added that whatever errors and shortcomings may be found in this material are entirely the authors' own responsibility.

H. G. H.
F. S.

Contents

The numbers refer to sections, not to pages.

Infinitive and *-ing* Form	1–74
Syntactic functions	1–2
-ing form or infinitive?	3–15
Idiomatic uses of the *-ing* form	16
The infinitive after interrogatives	17–18
English: infinitive – German: relative clause	19–20
The infinitive equivalent to an adverbial clause	21–23
Active versus passive infinitive	24 27
The pro-infinitive	28–29
The split infinitive	30–31
The infinitive group	32–45
For + infinitive group	46–50
With(out) + (pro)noun + infinitive	51–52
Present versus perfect infinitive	53–56
-ing constructions equivalent to subordinate clauses	57–62
Misrelated *-ing* constructions	63
The (pro)noun + *-ing* construction	64–66
The *-ing* form with a passive meaning	67
The absolute *-ing* construction	68–69
The *-ing* form: miscellaneous exercises	70–74
The Tenses	75–150
The simple present	75–76
Present simple versus present progressive	77–92
The simple past	93–95
Past simple versus past progressive	96–98
Simple versus progressive form	99–106
Present perfect and past tense	107–113
Present perfect simple versus present perfect progressive	114–118
The simple and progressive forms of *live*	119
Structures with *since*	120–121
Present perfect: miscellaneous exercises	122
The past perfect	123–124
Ways of expressing futurity	125–141
Conditional sentences	142–147
Reported speech	148–150
The Auxiliaries	151–207
Have	151–155
Need and *dare*	156–157

Can, could, was/were able to	158–161
May, might	162–168
Can, could, may, and *might* compared	169–171
Will, would	172–174
Shall, be to	175–178
Shall versus *will*	179
Should	180–182
Should versus *would*	183
Used to and *would*	184–187
Ought to, must	188–189
Must, should, need, ought to, have to, and *be to* compared	190–191
Können	192
Dürfen	193
Wollen	194
Sollen	195
Müssen	196
Werden	197
Brauchen	198
Miscellaneous exercises	199
Tags and short responses	200–205
Miscellaneous uses of auxiliaries	206–207
The Subjunctive	208–209
Irregular Verbs	210–211
The Passive	212–218
The Genitive	219–221
Number Form of Nouns	222–224
Concord	225–234
Gender	235–236
The Definite Article	237–246
The Indefinite Article	247–257
–self Pronouns	258–259
Possessive Adjectives	260–261
Interrogatives	262–263
Relative Clauses	264–266
Case Problems	267
Some and *Any*	268–269
It and *Es*	270–271
Comparison	272–275
Adjectives in Noun Function	276–277
Adverbs	278–288
Word Order	289–293
Prepositions	294–307

Infinitive & -ing Form

1 Determine the syntactic functions of the infinitives in the following sentences.

1. *To do* nothing but one's duty can be a demoralizing process.
2. My problem is *to get* home.
3. The firm decided *to seek* expert opinion.
4. I wonder how *to do* it.
5. I ached *to talk* to someone about what had happened.
6. It's time *to go* now.
7. They can't possibly make ends meet with a family *to educate*.
8. She was afraid *to go out* alone.
9. *To make* matters worse, the tide came in and the men were soon knee-deep in water.
10. The agreement called for a survey of existing housing, the landlords *to pay* all expenses.

2 Determine the syntactic functions of the -*ing* forms in the following sentences.

1. *Lying* there in the sun gave me a quiet contentment.
2. All he cared about was *getting* the job done.
3. I intend *going* into politics.
4. How do you think I can write these letters with the children *jumping* about all the time?
5. He felt embarrassed at *being* the centre of attention.
6. I was looking forward to *seeing* her again.
7. There is no hope of *curing* him.
8. After *watching* the ceremony, we went to the local for a couple of beers.
9. When *buying* a hat, you should also consider the price.
10. *Being* intelligent as well as unscrupulous, he is very dangerous.
11. *Considering* his age, he has done very well.
12. Thus passed a month, each day *making* life more and more unbearable.
13. They came *hurrying* into the garden.
14. Your words do not sound *encouraging*.
15. Can you smell something *burning*?
16. She went out by the door *leading* to the lounge.
17. A *falling* branch startled the boy.

3 Compare the following.

1. a) *Going* to fairs and markets was one of his favourite pastimes.
   b) *To go* to America is one of my great ambitions.
2. a) *Speaking* in public was always rather difficult for him.
   b) *To speak* was impossible for him when he saw his hope ruined.
3. a) It was very nice *having* you to tea last Wednesday.
   b) It's nice *to see* you again.

Infinitive & -ing Form

4. a) I always hated *being* a nobody.
   b) I hate *to trouble* you at this hour, but I urgently need your help.
5. a) I prefer *looking* after my own clothes.
   b) Come and play tennis with me. – No, thanks, I'd prefer *to stay* at home.
6. a) For a time he tried *writing* novels for a livelihood.
   b) One of the older boys tried *to explain* the meaning of the word.
7. a) He stopped *eating*.
   b) He stopped *to eat*.
8. a) This meant *converting* merchant ships to carry fuel and ammunition.
   b) I mean *to work* harder in future.
9. a) I can't remember *being* drunk.
   b) He even remembered *to get* some apples for the sauce.
10. a) We propose *leaving* at noon.
    b) We propose *to make* a change.
11. a) She set her glass down and began *looking* at him intently.
    b) He began *to realize* that he had made a mistake.
12. a) She has learnt *cooking*.
    b) She has learnt *to cook*.

4 *-ing* form or infinitive? – Say in which cases either form would be possible.

1. We meant (come) home early. 2. She remembers (see) him go out of the house. 3. Rembrandt's "Nightwatch" is a picture I always enjoy (look) at. 4. Washington set about (tot) up the results of the summit conference. 5. Now please stop (say) wild things you don't mean. 6. I merely try (do) my duty. 7. I hate (leave) you alone on this occasion. 8. I decided (play) to the limit. 9. Did you remember (take) your iron tonic? 10. After a day or two she had ceased (feel) even a flicker of surprise at her situation. 11. It's no good (have) teachers who let the girls get saucy with them. 12. The children adored (make) the map. 13. Rodney, don't bother (say) good-bye. 14. There was nothing left for me but to try (beg). 15. One could live continuously in a city of a quarter million and miss (see) certain people for years. 16. I couldn't bear (go) back to that place again. 17. In due course the secret police contrived (extract) from him the rest of his political history. 18. I disdained (ask) too many questions about George's affairs. 19. So you really propose (go) back to your parish work. 20. He detested (be) alone.

5 *-ing* form or infinitive?

1. Quite soon they discontinued (talk) and gave their attention to eating. 2. Have you finished (repair) the central heating? 3. Gordon contrived (work) off his shoes and socks without sitting up. 4. He affected (have) forgotten the poem Ravelton was speaking of. 5. He abhors (be) on the losing side. 6. I can't afford (shave) every morning. 7. He's late. Unfortunately this means (wait). 8. I like (be) alone. 9. Remember (bring) a parcel of washing next time you come. 10. I

Infinitive & -ing Form

didn't even bother (look) at him.   11. I didn't stop (thank) her.   12. He hates (get) letters nowadays.   13. I told the boss that I could not continue (work) without an advance on my wages.   14. The educated man prefers (keep) things as they are.   15. Once or twice, Joyce had debated (start) a small dress business.   16. She didn't plan (tell) us about whatever she had done.   17. Whatever he was doing, he always stopped (listen) to his grandchildren.   18. The results are very disappointing, I regret (say).   19. Any guard who saw him would commence (shoot).   20. She could not resist (give) presents to her friends.

-ing form or infinitive? [6]

1. He had to practise (draw) others into the conversation.   2. She enjoyed (have) people for dinner.   3. He didn't hesitate (place) the responsibility on the young doctor.   4. I hate (quarrel) anyway.   5. Sex never ceases (fascinate) me.   6. I hate (think) that tomorrow we'll be back in New York.   7. I adore (lunch) with you.   8. The stranger burst out (laugh).   9. Do you resent (have) to pay taxes?   10. He could remember (be) on the merry-go-round, (rise) and (fall) on the wooden horse with the clanging, tinny music in his ears.   11. To make life easier for the cops, the report suggested (take) away their responsibility for arresting quiet drunks who are not being offensive.   12. I never learnt (use) a typewriter.   13. I dread (think) of what may happen.   14. He had neglected (bring) old gloves of his own.   15. I'd love (talk) to him.   16. The contractor omitted (sign) the paper.   17. They chose (boycott) the conference.   18. At first he denied (be) in the car, but later he admitted it.   19. I value (be) independent.   20. She was unable to resist (tell) him the news.

-ing form or infinitive? [7]

1. I shall never forget (meet) her at the party.   2. She must have forgotten (lend) him the money, since she has offered him some more.   3. The President declined (characterize) his moves as "escalation".   4. She had arranged (introduce) Bertrand to him during the weekend.   5. It was hard work (walk) up the dry sandy path to the Welches' house.   6. He tried (open) the bathroom door; it was again locked.   7. He considered (use) soap as a pomatum, but decided against it.   8. Stop (push) and (pull) me about.   9. His wife endeavoured (inject) a more friendly note into the proceedings.   10. Some people yearn (prove) themselves unprejudiced.   11. Dixon, who was beginning (do) what he'd have described as "feeling his age", sat down in a chair and began (drink) his drink and (smoke) a cigarette.   12. She doesn't like (say) certain things in front of you.   13. How would you like (go) away with me?   14. I always like (meet) people who are interested in ballet.   15. Slowly and inefficiently, she started (look) for her handbag.   16. He dared not risk (appear) inquisitive.   17. I wish you'd quit (worry) about money.   18. I do not relish (be) awakened in the middle of the night.   19. A massive 80 per cent of American voters oppose (go) to war with

Infinitive & -ing Form

China. 20. He saw fit (compare) his arrival in Quebec with his return to the France his Anglo-Saxon allies had just liberated in World War II.

8 *-ing* form or infinitive?

1. He was considering (take) the bedside table downstairs. 2. A study of the egg and bacon and tomatoes opposite him made him decide to postpone (eat) any himself. 3. How in God's name do you expect me to finish my story if you keep (interrupt) me all the time? 4. For a moment he contemplated (dash) downstairs and (attempt) to make a bolt for it. 5. Conan Doyle volunteered (serve) in the Boer War. 6. I can't keep on (tell) him – it just goes in one ear and out the other. 7. I used to like (watch) Stanley play the piano. 8. I couldn't help (regard) her remark as a compliment. 9. I didn't mean (make) so much trouble. 10. "I write by ear," explained Groucho Marx in a letter to E. B. White. "I tried (write) with the typewriter but I found it too unwieldy. I then tried (dictate) to my secretary but after some months of futility I realized that she, too, was unwieldy."

9 Study the following examples.

1. There is no *hope of curing* him.
2. Are you in the *habit of smoking*?
3. They expressed their *surprise at seeing* him there.
4. But they had been hindered by the *objection* of farmers *to providing* suitable land.
5. He could not resist the rare *opportunity of writing* himself into the story.
6. Ellen had not had much *opportunity of doing* her duty by Daisy.
7. He wrote to him, saying that he would welcome the *opportunity of publishing* some further works from his pen.
8. Now had come her *opportunity of giving* the two rooms a good dusting.
9. It was one more *opportunity to keep* the ball rolling.
10. Someone who shares your news interest will welcome the *opportunity to get* Newsweek at a special low rate.
11. She took the *opportunity to ask* for asylum.
12. He would have no *opportunity to inform* the police.
13. I had no *intention of flying* to the Congo.
14. It's my *intention to buy* a new car.
15. He alone had had the *chance of making* money.
16. I didn't get the *chance to say* anything.
17. Neither the U.N. nor any other great power has the *right to dictate* the peace terms to this country.
18. No *attempt to escape* was made.
19. Dixon studied the Callaghan girl, despite his *determination to notice* nothing more about her.
20. We will not move back an inch until our opponents show their *willingness to begin* negotiating directly with us.

Infinitive & -ing Form

10 Supply the correct form of the verb in brackets, i.e. either the infinitive preceded by the particle *to*, or the *-ing* form preceded by a preposition. Point out cases which admit of more than one correct solution.

1. If you've got hair, you have a much better chance (get) through the receptionist to the boss. 2. She might seize eagerly on the chance (revenge) herself. 3. I have a great dislike (share) lodgings. 4. It isn't my habit (discuss) official business with my subordinates. 5. He isn't in the habit (discuss) official business with his subordinates. 6. Chaplin misses no opportunity (show) off Miss Loren's Olympian beauty. 7. There are other ways (bring) pressure to bear. 8. Thorne, a busy man, seldom had occasion (leave) London. 9. Did you have a chance (say) a few words to the Governor tonight? 10. You cannot deny me the right (leave) the country. 11. She could not resist the temptation (loiter) for a moment. 12. Only one thing was left, the instinct (survive). 13. I have no hesitation (tell) you that all preparations are now being made. 14. We shall be given an opportunity (strike) a mighty blow against the accursed tyrant. 15. He had the reputation (be) a habitual drunkard. 16. Our meeting gave us an opportunity (get) acquainted with each other. 17. That's not the way (do) it. 18. There were days when she pined for the courage (speak) to strangers in the street. 19. They did him the honour (dine) aboard. 20. If this country has the right (exist), it also has the right to the means (continue) that existence.

11 Infinitive preceded by *to*, or *-ing* form preceded by preposition?

1. He felt a little weak at the knees and an urge (go) to the lavatory. 2. On my next visit to London I took the opportunity (have) a talk with him. 3. He had not the slightest intention (do) any more work. 4. Most of them took the opportunity (talk) freely. 5. I am at a loss (explain) this phenomenon. 6. Everywhere we have the misfortune (be) despised and misunderstood. 7. I had taken the precaution (buy) a small bottle of whisky. 8. At Berkeley, students have a knack (get) what they want. 9. They gave him a good chance (survive) the vagaries of the revolution. 10. When do you think you'll get a chance (read) the novel? 11. He had an excellent chance (be) beaten. 12. Some of us feel the impulse (benefit) humanity. 13. There is no way (support) them properly. 14. He had difficulty (find) paper to write on. 15. There is no point (rub) the government the wrong way. 16. He is on his way (become) a celebrity. 17. I was supposed to be studying literature with a view (become) a teacher. 18. Congress showed little inclination (waste) time on the civil rights bill. 19. For Great Britain there is no genuine alternative (become) a European nation. 20. She expressed the wish (be) buried quietly.

12 Infinitive preceded by *to*, or *-ing* form preceded by preposition?

1. After getting a black eye, he was ashamed (show) his face. 2. I should be ashamed (be) caught laughing at anything connected with the Bible. 3. How

Infinitive & -ing Form

many children are capable (recognize) parental greatness? 4. No one wants to inflict embarrassment and emotional pain on dying patients, and so people are chary (embark) on frank discussion of what the dying feel or suspect. 5. Our Gemini astronauts made us proud (be) Americans. 6. A man should be ashamed (cry). 7. I'm naturally anxious (strike) while the iron is hot. 8. Wilson, for the moment, was dead-set (carry) on, regardless. 9. The children are very keen (go) to Sunday school again. 10. They aren't so keen (show) their ignorance. 11. Reade felt embarrassed (be) the centre of attention. 12. We are interested (know) just what means you used to produce the cover of the special issue. 13. I'm certainly interested (meet) artists like him.

13 Infinitive preceded by *to*, or *-ing* form preceded by preposition?

1. I'm fortunate (have) a cellar here containing many fine wines. 2. It's my experience that most newspapermen are not averse (think) of themselves as key figures. 3. He did not know that he was committed (buy) the new house and (desert) the ancient comfort of Bergheim. 4. He was destined (live) his adult life in the shadow of his aggressive father. 5. The judge was not disposed (believe) the witness . 6. I'm entitled (know) what's going on. 7. She was given (wear) semi-transparent dresses, with very little underneath them. 8. He's so drunk he's liable (choke). 9. The police were loath (accept) the testimony of such unreliable witnesses. 10. You are prone (be) too hasty with your answers. 11. During the past fortnight they had found him increasingly slack in his work and even more prone (lie) than usual. 12. He spoke sharply, with far more heat than he was wont (speak). 13. The prisoner pleaded guilty (have) acted as a receiver.

14 Infinitive preceded by *to*, or *-ing* form preceded by preposition?

1. His wife is accustomed (spend) more on herself in one week than he earns in six months. 2. I am not a man accustomed (live) on dreams. 3. We called upon a solicitor accustomed (handle) such matters. 4. I realized that I was totally unaccustomed (be) really alone. 5. We've got to accustom ourselves (run) a deficit budget. 6. His years of training as a mathematician had accustomed him (solve) problems. 7. I admit (have) a small soft spot in my heart for our mayor. 8. Radio broadcasts warned other women to be on their guard against the smooth-talking, harmless-appearing De Salvo, who confessed (strangle) thirteen women and (rape) and (assault) hundreds more. 9. She had consented (receive) her new admirer the following afternoon in her apartment. 10. One night she worked late and they got (talk). 11. A total materialist never gets around (read) Blake. 12. I'm looking forward (go) to Paris. 13. The paper came out with an editorial fulminating against employers who stooped (give) their servant girls false characters. 14. She testified (see) the accused man in the neighbourhood of the cottage. 15. He devoted all his energies (learn) English. 16. You had far better see (get) your dinner. 17. She has taken (study) Egyptian hieroglyphs as a hobby.

Infinitive & -ing Form

15 Supply the appropriate form of the verb in brackets, i.e. either infinitive preceded by *to*, or the *-ing* form preceded by *of*. Then, try to paraphrase the construction with *afraid*.

1. The morning paper said that as a result of the recent murders quite a lot of women were afraid (go) out alone.   2. In the thirties, British businessmen were afraid (invest) in Europe.   3. Soon she will probably marry someone who isn't afraid (kiss) her.   4. "We are not afraid (fight) and we are not afraid (die)," he shouted defiantly.   5. She was afraid (take) a sleeping pill, in case news should come.   6. Their motors simply whizzed through the streets at top speed, as though they were afraid (be) attacked.   7. I was afraid (be) shot at.   8. He hurried behind her, afraid (lose) her in some shop.   9. We're afraid (offend) him.   10. I was afraid (wake) my sister, so I did not use the phone.   11. Trowman looked about self-consciously, afraid (be) seen with the condemned, worried by herd verdict. It was possible to pity Trowman, feel a bit braver in his presence, so weak, human, fallible, afraid (have) an opinion was he.   12. Nancy, who had been afraid (fly) coming up, was the one who insisted on returning by plane.   13. He was afraid (fly), afraid (think) of the Atlantic thirty thousand feet below us, and only the greater fear of pursuit by phantom detectives, with serpents in their hair and tears of blood in their eyes, persuaded him to risk his life in a machine which, to a simple pragmatical person like myself, seemed eminently safe.   14. He, who had risked his life all the time, was suddenly afraid (fly).   15. Many, many people, even experienced travellers, are still secretly afraid (fly).   16. I was afraid (die) and I was afraid of disgrace.   17. He was afraid (fail), (not measure) up to expectation; he was afraid (be) afraid; and he was desperately afraid, above all things, (be) seen, (be) known to be afraid.   18. "You're deranged, I suppose," she said carefully, speaking to hurt. "Probably suffering from some psychosomatic form of impotence, and afraid (reveal) it." – "I'd certainly be afraid (reveal) it when you were about," he said.   19. "Who's afraid (say) anything openly?" – "I'm not in the least afraid (say) things openly."

16 Translate the following sentences into German.

1. The sun was near setting.   2. How about having a rest now?   3. As to keeping his promise, he didn't even think of it.   4. It was all very close to being a miracle.   5. He is past praying for.   6. The criminal was past caring.   7. Besides driving and looking after the car, there will also be housework for you to do.   8. Cleveland came close to electing a Negro mayor last month.   9. Are any of the traditional problems of philosophy any nearer to being solved by us than they were by the Greeks?   10. The answer was not long in coming.   11. For the present there was nothing doing.   12. We were late getting here.   13. There was a great deal of shouting and screaming and banging of doors.   14. There was no knowing what she wanted.   15. I don't feel like swimming today.   16. His horses were an excellent pair, and they looked like winning.   17. All this wealth is yours for the taking.   18. The money is yours for the asking.   19. That beautiful blue dress

Infinitive & -ing Form

must have taken some finding. 20. He is a clever rogue, if ever there was one, and he'll take some catching. 21. She does a lot of reading.

17 The infinitive after interrogatives like *how, what, when, where,* and *whether.* – Study the following examples and translate them into German.

1. They argued about *whether to go* to Buffalo before spending the winter in Florida.
2. There was a debate about *where to stop.*
3. None of them knew *what to do.*
4. I told my secretary *which calls to let through.*
5. He seemed to have an instinct that told him *when to put on* an appearance of industry.

18 Sentences for translation.

1. Bitte raten Sie mir, welche Schritte ich unternehmen soll. 2. Meine Frau weiß nicht, ob sie den Fisch braten oder kochen soll. 3. Ich weiß nicht, warum ich diesem doch offensichtlich böswilligen Ratschlag folgen soll. 4. Ich lernte Auto fahren, und das Fahren wurde meine Leidenschaft. 5. Ich wußte nicht, ob ich ihr glauben sollte oder nicht. 6. Das Problem, wie man die Fehler der Vergangenheit wiedergutmachen soll, ist nicht unser einziges Problem. 7. Ich bin noch im Zweifel, ob ich hingehen soll oder nicht. 8. Sie wußte nicht, was für Bücher sie John zum Geburtstag schenken sollte. 9. Ich weiß nicht recht, was ich vorschlagen soll. 10. Ich weiß nicht, was ich davon halten soll. 11. Dann war da auch noch die Frage des Abreisetermins. 12. Warum bringst du ihm nicht das Boxen bei? 13. Ein guter Redner weiß, wann er aufhören muß. 14. Plötzlich wußte er, was er tun mußte und wie er es tun mußte. 15. Ich wußte nicht, ob ich ihr trauen konnte. 16. Sie konnte gut mit Männern umgehen und wußte genau, wann man sie unterhalten und wann man sie in Ruhe lassen mußte. 17. Das erste Problem war, wo er seinen Koffer lassen sollte. 18. Man konnte sich noch nicht einmal darüber einigen, wann und wo man die Tagung abhalten sollte. 19. Die Frage, wen man zur Hochzeit einladen sollte, war sehr delikat. 20. Damals debattierte das Parlament gerade die Frage, ob man nun die Todesstrafe abschaffen sollte oder nicht. 21. Draußen stritten sie sich, wessen Wagen sie nehmen sollten.

19 English: infinitive – German: relative clause. – Study the following examples and translate them into German.

1. We could see nothing at which to shoot.
2. Before long he was able to buy a car in which to cover his sales territory in the south of England.
3. You have five minutes in which to make up your mind.
4. He had nothing else with which to occupy himself.

Infinitive & -ing Form

5. I had nobody to talk to.
6. Almost any situation is bearable if you have a home to go back to.
7. I admit this isn't a hopeful age to write poetry in.
8. In the same ward is a small Pakistani boy, who has no mother to visit him.
9. He decided that Tom and I should be the first to disappear.
10. Miller told me that you were the one to first mention my name.

Sentences for translation. **20**

1. Lord Byron hinterließ keinen Sohn, der seinen Titel hätte erben können. 2. Ich gebe Ihnen einige Muster, unter denen sie wählen können. 3. Ich werde gewissenhaft alles zu vermeiden suchen, was ihn beleidigen könnte. 4. Ein Gast war besonders willkommen, wenn er ein paar Anekdoten mitbrachte, mit denen er seine Tischgenossen unterhalten konnte. 5. Dieses Mädchen ist das zweite Kind, das nach der Impfung starb. 6. Sie möchte nur jemanden, mit dem sie sich unterhalten kann. 7. Er war der einzige, der den Erzherzog mit „Durchlaucht" anredete. 8. Man gab Lydia ein Bett, auf das sie ihren Strohsack legen konnte. 9. Sie sind vielleicht der Mann, der mein Nachfolger wird. 10. Das Lateinische ist eine Sprache, in der man herrlich Liebesgedichte schreiben kann. 11. Er wählte zehn Männer aus, die ihn auf seiner Expedition begleiten sollten. 12. Er war der einzige im Kollegium, der einen Bart trug. 13. Er stellte ein paar neue Redakteure ein, die der Zeitschrift einen munteren und etwas beißenden Ton geben sollten. 14. Man betrachtete den Engländer als jemanden, dem man in jeder Situation vertrauen konnte. 15. Soll ich dir ein Taxi bestellen, in dem du nach Hause fahren kannst? 16. Als er in London ankam, hatte er nur noch etwa dreißig Schilling, mit denen er bis zum folgenden Montag auskommen mußte. 17. Seine Frau ließ es sich angelegen sein, sich für alles, was mit seiner Arbeit zusammenhing, zu interessieren. 18. Ich gebe dir ein Buch, das du auf der Reise lesen kannst. 19. Er versuchte, Worte zu finden, mit denen er seinen verzweifelten Freund aufmuntern konnte. 20. Wir dürfen mit Sicherheit annehmen, daß Miss Young eine Person ist, die Respekt verlangt. 21. Man wird versuchen, Zeugen zu finden, die dich identifizieren können. 22. Rodney war immer derjenige gewesen, der die offiziellen Entscheidungen traf. 23. Er stellte ein paar Männer ein, die seine Frau beobachten sollten. 24. Er ist kein Mann, der den Kopf in den Sand steckt. 25. Er war nicht der einzige Berliner Buchhändler, der Zuflucht in England fand. 26. Ich wäre der letzte, der dir daraus einen Vorwurf machen würde. 27. Der alte Kapitän war nicht der Mann, der vor einer Gefahr zurückschreckte. 28. Das einzig Vernünftige, was man tun konnte, war, ihr einen Brief zu schreiben. 29. Er ist nicht der Typ, der mit sich handeln läßt. 30. Der erste der Zeugen, der vernommen wurde, war Robert Allwood.

The infinitive equivalent to an adverbial clause. – Study the following examples **21**
and translate them into German.

1. I am deeply sorry to be the one to have to break such tidings to you.

Infinitive & -ing Form

2. It made the boys laugh to see the girl cry.
3. His heart sickened to think that he had only fivepence halfpenny in the world.
4. Nobby woke her up to tell her that he had got tea ready.
5. I'm going early so as to get a good seat.
6. How careless he must be to cross the road without looking.
7. Henry can't be such a bloody fool as to do a thing like that.
8. They are too intelligent to agree in advance to tie their hands.
9. He once went so far as to praise the general as "the greatest statesman of our time".
10. The light was bright enough to read by.
11. He awoke to find himself in a strange room.
12. To judge by his outward appearance, he must be rich.
13. He looked at the clock as if to indicate that the interview was finished.
14. Who the hell are you to give orders here?

22 Sentences for translation.

1. Die Polizei erschien, um das Haus zu durchsuchen. 2. Wer sind Sie denn, daß Sie sich in meine Angelegenheiten einmischen? 3. Ich muß wirklich ein Sonntagskind sein, daß ich einem so großzügigen Menschen begegnet bin. 4. Was für eine hohe Meinung die Reporter von seiner Allwissenheit haben müssen, daß sie alle Antworten auf ihre Fragen so sorgfältig aufschreiben. 5. Wenn man ihn so sprechen hört, sollte man denken, er habe die Hälfte seines Lebens in Australien verbracht. 6. Wenn man den Mann so sah, wie er dasaß, schien es, als wäre er vorzeitig gealtert. 7. Es wäre keine Übertreibung, wenn man hinzufügte, daß alle freien Völker an dieser Dankesschuld teilhaben. 8. Du hältst mich wohl für einen schrecklichen Dummkopf, weil ich dies nicht erraten habe? 9. Der Verbrecher war so unvorsichtig, daß er in die Falle ging, die ihm die Polizei gestellt hatte. 10. Oft muß er am Essen sparen, damit er seine Ausgaben für Zigaretten bestreiten kann. 11. Sein Betragen war so kalt, daß es fast unmenschlich war. 12. Ich bin doch nicht ein solches Rindvieh, daß ich alles glaube, was er mir sagt. 13. Er ist doch nicht so dumm, daß er sich ins eigene Fleisch schneidet. 14. Sie streckte die Hand aus, als wollte sie zwischen die beiden Streitenden treten. 15. Es ist schön, wenn man eine Uhr als Geschenk bekommt.

23 Translate into German.

1. The little girl opened her eyes to find herself alone in bed, and started screaming. 2. He woke at ten to say he felt well and was hungry. 3. He came into the parlour to discover that the guests had begun to arrive. 4. They entered the house to find Emily Prout already installed behind the silver kettle in the drawing room. 5. Late that night I woke to find Jenny bent over me, watching me anxiously. 6. I emerged from the elevator on the twenty-third floor to find myself in a thickly carpeted corridor, on both sides of which were doors painted in a great variety of pastel colours.

Infinitive & -ing Form

Active and passive infinitive. – Sentences for observation.

24

1. a) Pictures are not the only things *to see* at Florence.
   b) A few snowdrops were the only things *to be seen*.
2. a) There is nothing *to do*.
   b) There is nothing *to be done*.
3. a) There is a lot of work *to do*.
   b) There is a lot of work *to be done*.
4. a) There is nothing *to fear*.
   b) There is nothing *to be feared*.
5. a) Who is *to blame* for starting the fire?
   b) Who is *to be blamed* for starting the fire?
6. a) Office building *to let* on temporary tenancy.
   b) Office building *to be let* at moderate rent to approved tenant.

Active or passive infinitive?

25

1. It is to (doubt) whether he knows that. 2. This house is to (let). 3. This house is to (let) or to (sell). 4. He saw everything there was to (see). 5. Nothing is to (see). 6. There is no time to (lose). 7. His behaviour was not to (blame). 8. The reason is not far to (seek). 9. That is not fit to (use). 10. The rabbit is ready to (eat). 11. The rabbit is cooked and ready to (eat). 12. The pain seemed too great to (bear). 13. These boxes are not strong enough to (use) as a platform. 14. There is a lot to (do) yet. 15. That was not to (foresee). 16. The book is pleasant to (read). 17. Some girls are jolly to (watch) when they run. 18. The young stowaway was to (pity) rather than to (condemn). 19. It is an awkward door to (open). 20. That remains to (see). 21. The next thing to (consider) was food. 22. His language is not fit to (repeat).

Sentences for translation.

26

1. Es war ganz offensichtlich, daß ihm nicht zu trauen war. 2. Sein Notizbuch war nirgendwo zu sehen. 3. Sein Notizbuch war nicht schwer zu finden. 4. Kein Ton war zu hören. 5. Keine Menschenseele war zu sehen. 6. Bestimmungen sind dafür da, daß man sie umgeht. 7. Sie war nirgendwo zu finden. 8. Sie war leicht zu finden. 9. Es bleibt noch viel zu tun. 10. Das war zu erwarten. 11. Das Essen ließ nichts zu wünschen übrig. 12. Die Wunden des Krieges heilen langsam. 13. Sie war wunderschön anzuschauen. 14. Es war nie langweilig, für ihn zu arbeiten. 15. Mit ihm ist schwer auszukommen. 16. Das ist nicht leicht zu erklären. 17. Das läßt sich leichter sagen als tun. 18. Das ist leichter gesagt als getan. 19. Mit Bettina wird man leichter reden können als mit Lydia. 20. Miss Summerfield ist furchtbar schwer hinters Licht zu führen. 21. Ich habe noch nie eine Frau getroffen, zu der man so schwer nein sagen konnte. 22. Ich weiß, daß es unmöglich ist, mit mir zusammenzuleben. 23. Man kann sich mit ihr interessant unterhalten. 24. Sie ist eine Frau, mit der man sich interessant

Infinitive & -ing Form

unterhalten kann. 25. Auf dem Ausstellungsgelände gab es alles mögliche zu sehen. 26. Da wird sich wohl nichts machen lassen. 27. Es war keine Zeit zu verlieren. 28. Man konnte nur eines tun. 29. Es waren massenhaft Wohnungen zu haben. 30. Dem läßt sich nichts hinzufügen. 31. In einem Augenblick wie diesem kann man nur eines tun. 32. In diesem Teil der Stadt ist kaum ein Baum oder eine Blume zu sehen. 33. Es gibt noch andere, an die wir denken müssen. 34. Ich habe mit dir noch ein Hühnchen zu rupfen, und zwar ein großes! 35. Ich muß mich um meine eigenen Angelegenheiten kümmern. 36. Wenn es uns gelingt, die Küste zu erreichen, haben wir wenig zu befürchten. 37. Du mußt noch viel lernen. 38. Du brauchst dir um nichts Sorgen zu machen. 39. Wir haben heute was zu feiern. 40. Du tust so, als ob du etwas zu verbergen hättest. 41. Er äußert sich nur, wenn er etwas Wichtiges zu sagen hat. 42. Er hat ein Haus zu verkaufen. 43. Im Augenblick habe ich vier Zimmer zu vermieten. 44. Ich habe dem nicht das geringste hinzuzufügen. 45. Heutzutage gibt es für uns nicht viel zu lachen. 46. Wir dürfen keinen Augenblick verlieren. 47. An eine Heirat war noch nicht zu denken. 48. Er war schwer zufriedenzustellen. 49. Er sah alles, was es zu sehen gab. 50. Die Aussicht war zu schön, als daß man sie je vergessen könnte. 51. Sein Gesicht war so entsetzlich anzuschauen, daß ich unruhig wurde. 52. Sie sah ihn ziemlich erschrocken an und fragte, was zu tun sei. 53. Ein Bericht über dieses Ereignis ist in der zeitgenössischen Literatur zu finden. 54. Wir haben mehr als genug Platz in unserer Wohnung. 55. Hier ist nichts zu haben. 56. In dieser Zeit hatte es keine nennenswerten Ereignisse gegeben.

27 Please translate, using *blame*.

1. Ich habe genau so viel Schuld wie du. 2. Der Polizei kann man keine Vorwürfe machen. 3. Er war in keiner Weise an der Panne schuld. 4. Irgend jemand mußte man ja die Schuld geben, und da fiel die Wahl logischerweise auf mich.

28 The pro-infinitive. – Sentences for observation.

1. I hear you have decided to accept this position abroad. – Of course, I should be a fool not to.
2. Have you read his latest novel yet? – No, but I'm certainly going to.
3. Are you pouring out the tea, Mary? – Yes, Mother asked me to.
4. I shall lend him the money. – Will you allow me to advise you not to?

29 Sentences for translation.

1. Ich wollte nicht über Nacht bleiben, aber er bat mich darum. 2. Zeigen Sie mir bitte, wie man das macht. – Aber gerne. 3. Du kannst mit uns kommen, wenn du Lust hast. 4. Leider kann ich überhaupt nicht kommen. – Aber du hast es

Infinitive & -ing Form

doch versprochen. 5. Ich gehe morgen zu der Feier; wenigstens habe ich es vor. 6. Ich hörte ihn gestern abend seine Frau schlagen. – Nun, dazu hat er doch ein Recht! 7. Nicht gehorchen? Ich fürchte, du mußt es. 8. Er sieht nicht ein, warum die Leute nicht um Geld spielen sollten, wenn sie es wollen. 9. Du hast mir nicht einmal auf Wiedersehen gesagt. – Nein, das habe ich vergessen. 10. Warum hast du ihn nicht besucht, als du dort warst? – Dazu hatte ich keine Veranlassung.

The split infinitive. – Compare and discuss the following examples. | 30 |

1. I sincerely wish to apologize.
2. I wish to apologize sincerely.
3. I wish sincerely to apologize.
4. I wish to sincerely apologize.

Discuss the phenomenon of the "split infinitive" in the light of the following quotations. | 31 |

1. It takes a fresh eye to fully appreciate Delia.
2. It isn't good to always work so hard.
3. Had he managed to completely cover his own tracks?
4. The Resistance networks performed a vital task that was to greatly facilitate the insurrection.
5. We put shillings in a hat, and the first one correctly to guess the singer would collect the jackpot.
6. Are you so determined always to have your own way that you are ready to make a scene any time to get it?
7. Stewart hadn't had a chance really to size up the Navy Captain.
8. When I hear gentlemen say that politics ought to let business alone, I feel like inviting them to first consider whether business is letting politics alone.
9. You oughtn't to ever do anything too long. (Hemingway)
10. He was tall and solemnly handsome, and he never split an infinitive or a bottle. (Sinclair Lewis)
11. In the simple gorgeousness of the Nautilus Smart Set, Mrs Tredgold had petted Leora and laughed at her if she lacked a shoe buckle or split an infinitive. (Sinclair Lewis)
12. Word has somehow got around that the split infinitive is always wrong. This is of a piece with the outworn notion that it is always wrong to strike a lady. (James Thurber)
13. If you do not immediately suppress the person who takes it upon himself to lay down the law almost every day in your columns on the subject of literary composition, I will give up the "Chronicle". The man is a pedant, an ignoramus, an idiot and a self-advertising duffer. Your fatuous specialist ... is now beginning to rebuke "second-rate" newspapers for using such phrases as "to suddenly go" and "to boldly say". I ask you, Sir, to put this

Infinitive & -ing Form

man out ... without interfering with his perfect freedom of choice between "to suddenly go", "to go suddenly", and "suddenly to go" ... Set him adrift and try an intelligent Newfoundland dog in his place. (George Bernard Shaw in a letter to the "Chronicle", 1892)

14. The English-speaking world may be divided into (1) those who neither know nor care what a split infinitive is; (2) those who do not know, but care very much; (3) those who know and condemn; (4) those who know and approve; and (5) those who know and distinguish. (Fowler)
15. The issue of the split infinitive has been undergoing a gradual change. It may well be that fifty years from now the taboo will be dead. But for the present the careful writer will in general observe it and when necessary disregard it. He will disregard it not defiantly but boldly – boldly in the sure knowledge that he knows what he is doing and can convince the discriminating reader of the fact, boldly because he is aware that to do otherwise would be to fall into ambiguity or awkwardness. (Theodore M. Bernstein)

32 The infinitive group. – Sentences for observation and discussion.

1. He *urged her to be* careful. 2. He *instructed them to report* for duty as soon as they heard the siren. 3. This sort of thing *leads him to become* boastful. 4. We succeeded in *persuading the judge to impose* a light sentence. 5. I *left her to find out* herself. 6. The gravity of the situation *determined him to act* at once. 7. He waited until he *heard the lock snap*. 8. They had *seen several aircraft go up* from the island. 9. His wife *encouraged him to try* again. 10. They couldn't *induce the old lady to travel* again.

33 The infinitive group. – Sentences for observation and discussion.

1. I *want you to listen* to me for a moment. 2. You could *trust her to be* somewhere in the neighbourhood. 3. He *expects the project to move* slowly. 4. We *intend them to do* it. 5. It has long been standard practice to *require women to wear* bathing caps at communal swimming pools. 6. I *require you to help* me. 7. She had *supposed the bag he had brought with him to contain* certain little necessaries of civilized life. 8. *Tell Matthew to fetch* the tray. 9. If we *suffer this bill to pass*, we shall not know where we stand. 10. He said he *preferred me to wait*. 11. I *believe the whole thing to have* been prearranged. 12. You *know him to be* a hard-working man, don't you? 13. He held a match to the newspaper and *watched it burn*. 14. Clementine *observed Winston's impatience grow*. 15. He could *feel the knife touch* his skin. 16. The doctor did not *consider her to be* seriously ill. 17. The police *caused the grave to be* opened. 18. The experts *held calculus to be* too difficult for that age group. 19. She hated airplanes and did not *like her husband to fly*. 20. I do not *desire your Lordship to think* that this is the most important point I'm making.

Infinitive & -ing Form

34 The infinitive group. – Sentences for observation and discussion.

1. Surely, you would not *have me wear* such an awful hat? 2. He *had the children go* to bed early. 3. Would you *have the government control* our lives completely? 4. She likes to *have the house look* clean and tidy. 5. She simply would not *have him treat* the dog like that. 6. I simply cannot bear to *have you think* me impertinent. 7. You are likely to *have people steal* from you if you do not lock the door. 8. He had never *known Henry show* much interest in other people. 9. I *challenge you to prove* what you have just said. 10. They *dared me to jump* over the stream. 11. I *defy you to repeat* that phrase. 12. I did not *mean you to hear* it. 13. She *tempted the child to have* a little more dinner. 14. I will *thank you to mind* your own business. 15. Do you *trust your young daughters to go* to dance halls with any sort of men? 16. Dixon didn't *trust himself to speak*.

35 In which of the following sentences could the infinitive group be replaced by a subordinate clause?

1. They *requested me to be* silent. 2. I *recommend you not to irritate* your boss. 3. They *invited me to come* to their party. 4. They *implored him to give up* this dangerous plan. 5. He *ordered the men to retreat* into the basement. 6. Poverty *compelled him to do* the humblest manual work. 7. This drug *causes the heart to flutter*. 8. Sharply the coroner *bade Lizzie Cole stand down*. 9. Hunger *drove him to steal*. 10. The captives *entreated the savages not to kill* them. 11. I *helped him carry* the cocktails. 12. She *begged him not to work* too hard. 13. He *commanded his troops to lay down* their arms. 14. Their incomes *allow them to enjoy* more of the luxuries of life. 15. Advertising *induces people to buy*. 16. The authorities did not *wish the population to see* this depressing sight. 17. Everybody *acknowledges him to be* a genius. 18. The doctor *certified the cause of death to be* cerebral thrombosis. 19. He *signalled me to wait* for a moment. 20. The English *dislike their homes to be* conspicuous. 21. The stars have *declared you to be* my friend and guardian. 22. He *felt the whole plan to be* foolish. 23. They *advised him to stay*. 24. He *noticed a messenger summon* the adjutant out of the room to receive a telephone call. 25. I'll *have him return* the money tomorrow. 26. I *expect him to be* on time. 27. You must *admit the task to be* extremely difficult. 28. He *felt his veins fill* with pure happiness. 29. The situation *requires me to be* present. 30. The map will *enable you to find* the place.

36 Which of the following sentences can be transformed in the manner indicated?
They requested him to use his influence on my behalf.
→ *He was requested to use* his influence on my behalf.

1. They reported the enemy to be ten miles away. 2. Tradition states him to be a game warden. 3. They advised him to start at once. 4. In vain they begged her

Infinitive & -ing Form

to change her mind. 5. They preferred the Ministry not to take any decisive steps. 6. They wanted Charlie to come to Blackpool just for a couple of days. 7. They commanded the deserters to be shot. 8. They perceived the figure to be a woman. 9. They observed him smile cheerfully. 10. They had a funny thing happen to them last night. 11. They would like you to go up to the house and explain. 12. They prompted him to ask for a transfer to a new job. 13. They recommended him to consult Dr Abrahams. 14. They require a lawyer to help them. 15. They all supposed him to be in America. 16. They told the boy not to forget about the letters. 17. They asked him to fill in the form. 18. They let me listen to their discussions a number of times. 19. They gave her to understand that her services were no longer required. 20. They watched him push his way through the door and disappear down the stairs. 21. They had forbidden him to mention it in front of the children. 22. They made anyone accused of crimes under the cultural revolution read his confession to an assembly of workers. 23. They overheard Bennett ask his wife whether she was taking the night train. 24. They had never seen him do any kind of manual job before. 25. He felt the pavement tremble. 26. They noticed him enter the building. 27. They dared me to contradict them. 28. The ever worsening situation decided them to leave the country. 29. They defied him to find these principles unworthy of a decent citizen. 30. They wished the priest to impress upon his friends the futility of further bloodshed.

37 In which of the following sentences can the infinitive be replaced by the *-ing* form? What difference in meaning, if any, is there between the two forms?

1. She wants you *to fight* for her. 2. They felt themselves *to be* above the law. 3. He could feel his heart *begin* to thump inside his chest. 4. She was noticed *to tremble* slightly when the name of John Baxter was read from the address book. 5. I don't want you *to make* promises because you feel sorry for me. 6. We can't allow him *to become* a cripple for life. 7. Jim thought he had never seen her *look* so beautiful. 8. I overheard Mrs Busk *tell* her husband that Mary would very likely be staying with them for some time. 9. They must be made *to see* that it is too late now. 10. They watched him *walk* down the street and followed in the car. 11. That author always has his characters *do* foolish things. 12. The bombs were not intended *to hit* civilian targets. 13. He was seen *to shake* his head. 14. She had heard the key *turn* in the hall door. 15. They let him *have* his say. 16. I can't have you *go* home thinking I'm altogether irresponsible. 17. He denied this *to be* the case. 18. We guessed him *to be* the man we wanted. 19. You don't want Dad *to fall* into the wrong hands, do you? 20. I thought you *to be* a brave man. 21. I'd hate you *to go* away thinking I didn't trust you. 22. They like people *to think* they own the place.

Infinitive & -ing Form

Sentences for translation and observation. **38**

1. a) Ich sah ihn die Tür schließen.
   b) Ich sah, daß er die Tür schloß.
   c) Ich sah, wie er die Tür schloß.
   d) Ich sah, daß er die Tür geschlossen hatte.
2. a) Ich hörte Singen.
   b) Ich hörte ein Lied singen.
   c) Ich hörte den Vogel singen.
   d) Man hörte den Vogel singen.

Translate the following sentences, using an infinitive group wherever possible. **39**

1. Er bat mich, die Formulare für ihn auszufüllen. 2. Man erwartet von dir, daß du gute Arbeit leistest. 3. Es wird von dir erwartet, daß du gute Arbeit leistest. 4. Man kann nicht von mir erwarten, daß ich für diesen Lohn täglich zehn Stunden arbeite. 5. Ich stellte fest, daß ich vor dem Mikrophon äußerst nervös war. 6. Man stellte fest, daß ich vor dem Mikrophon äußerst nervös war. 7. Der General befahl seinen Panzern, das Feuer zu eröffnen. 8. Die Panzer erhielten Befehl, das Feuer zu eröffnen. 9. Der General befahl, das Feuer zu eröffnen. 10. Charles hielt ihn für einen Detektiv. 11. Er soll ein Detektiv sein. 12. Man sagte, er lebe ganz zurückgezogen auf dem Lande. 13. Die Polizei sagt, er lebe ganz zurückgezogen auf dem Lande. 14. Sag Jennifer, sie soll sich keine Sorgen machen. 15. Ich hasse es, wenn du so redest. 16. Ich hätte es vorgezogen, wenn Mildred nicht gekommen wäre. 17. Ich glaube, sie hätte es lieber, wenn ich dabei wäre. 18. Er will, daß du kommst und dich entschuldigst. 19. Wir wollen nicht, daß du dich erkältest.

Translate the following sentences, using an infinitive group wherever possible. **40**

1. Sie ließen sich ohne jeden Widerstand entwaffnen und gefangennehmen. 2. Sein Gewissen zwang ihn, die Wahrheit zu sagen. 3. Man zwang ihn, den Safe zu öffnen. 4. Man ließ die Menschen in den Lagern verhungern. 5. Die Menschen in den Lagern wurden dem Hungertod preisgegeben. 6. Er überließ es seiner Frau, mit den Gläubigern zu verhandeln. 7. Er wollte, daß seine Frau mit den Gläubigern verhandelte. 8. Sie brachte ihrem Sohn das Rechnen, Lesen und Schreiben bei, bevor er in die Schule kam. 9. Man sagt ihr nach, daß sie dem Gästezimmer nächtliche Besuche abstattet. 10. Die Nachbarn sagen ihr nach, daß sie dem Gästezimmer nächtliche Besuche abstattet. 11. Man sagt von ihm, daß er seine Mitarbeiter sehr anständig behandelt. 12. Sie soll jetzt in Amerika leben. 13. Sie warnte mich davor, dieses Thema in seiner Gegenwart anzurühren. 14. Sie verlangte von mir, daß ich dieses Thema in seiner Gegenwart anschnitt.

Infinitive & -ing Form

41 Translate the following sentences, using an infinitive group wherever possible.

1. Die Krankheit hatte dazu geführt, daß ihm das Schlucken Schwierigkeiten bereitete. 2. Was hat dich dazu veranlaßt, zur Polizei zu gehen? 3. Ich wünsche, daß meine Leiche eingeäschert wird. 4. Diese Männer werdet ihr nicht zum Reden bringen. 5. Wir werden es so einrichten, daß Tony sich um die Hunde kümmert. 6. Wir werden Tony dazu kriegen, daß er sich um die Hunde kümmert. 7. Wir werden Tony sagen, daß er sich um die Hunde kümmern soll. 8. Mary hat es nicht gern, wenn jemand betrunken ist. 9. Er hat es nicht gern, wenn irgend jemand an seine Sachen geht. 10. Wir wollen es nicht haben, daß ihr Sachen kauft, die ihr euch nicht leisten könnt. 11. Ich will nicht, daß du noch mehr Geld von mir borgst. 12. Wir wollen es nicht haben, daß ihr so etwas über uns sagt.

42 Translate the following sentences, using an infinitive group wherever possible.

1. Er hielt sie für unschuldig. 2. Er glaubte, sie sei unschuldig. 3. Er glaubte, sein Freund habe ihn unfair behandelt. 4. Er glaubte, sein Freund sei unfair behandelt worden. 5. Er glaubte, man habe ihn unfair behandelt. 6. Sie wurde allgemein für schuldig gehalten. 7. Ich schätze ihn auf Mitte dreißig. 8. Ich glaube, er ist abgereist. 9. Man nimmt an, daß er abgereist ist. 10. Ich nehme an, daß er das Geld gestohlen hat. 11. Sie bildete sich ein, sie sei krank. 12. Ich wußte, daß er ein Lügner war.

43 Translate the following sentences, using an infinitive group wherever possible.

1. Er fühlte, wie der Boden unter seinen Füßen zitterte. 2. Ich fühlte, daß etwas nicht in Ordnung war. 3. Bemerkte jemand, daß der Dieb das Haus verließ? 4. Sie hörte, wie die Tür zuschlug. 5. Ich hörte ihn die ganze Nacht über rufen. 6. Jack hörte, wie sie das Geschirr wegräumte. 7. Man sah, daß seine Hände zitterten, als er die Seiten umblätterte. 8. Ich werde lediglich den anderen beim Spielen zuschauen. 9. Schau mal, wie das Pferd springt! 10. Er mußte dort sitzen und zuhören, wie andere Leute sich unterhielten.

44 Translate the following sentences, using an infinitive group wherever possible.

1. Ich werde veranlassen, daß er das Geld morgen zurückgibt. 2. Ich werde ihm sagen, daß er das Geld morgen zurückgeben soll. 3. Ich werde ihn zwingen, das Geld morgen zurückzugeben. 4. Ich werde vorschlagen, daß er das Geld morgen zurückgibt. 5. Ich werde ihn dazu bringen, daß er das Geld morgen zurückgibt. 6. Man wird ihn dazu veranlassen, das Geld morgen zurückzugeben. 7. Er soll das Geld morgen zurückgeben.

45 Translate the following sentences, using an infinitive group wherever possible.

1. Sie gab ihm zu verstehen, daß sie sich ärgerte. 2. Seine Familie hatte es nie erlebt, daß er um Geld bat. 3. Von mindestens einem Schiff weiß man, daß es

Infinitive & -ing Form

gesunken ist. 4. Er sagte, ihm sei etwas Merkwürdiges passiert. 5. Eines Nachts brach ihm ein Dieb in seinen Laden ein. 6. Lassen sie ihn zeitig kommen. 7. Sie ließ ihren Freund die Getränke bezahlen.

46 *For* + infinitive group. – Study the following examples and state in what syntactic functions *for* + infinitive group is used.

1. *For any doctor to take drugs* is bad enough.
2. The German custom is *for men to wear wedding rings* as well.
3. She asked *for it to be repeated*.
4. I want very much *for my son to be happier* than I have been.
5. Now was the time *for him to act*.
6. It was well known that there was a tendency *for "whitewashing" to occur*.
7. It seemed unnatural *for a girl to be so accurate*.
8. It seems funny *for someone to come back up here* after living in London.
9. He stood aside *for the others to pass*.
10. He rang the bell *for me to come down*.
11. *For education to be effective*, its chief work must be to build up character.

47 Compare the following.

1. a) He watched *somebody pass* in the street.
   b) He watched *for somebody to pass* in the street.
2. a) He asked *the boy to stay* a few days longer.
   b) He asked *for the boy to stay* a few days longer.
3. a) I want *my son to be* a great man.
   b) I want very much *for my son to be* a great man.

48 Sentences for translation.

1. Isn't that an awfully good piece of verse for a girl her age to write? 2. It was a painful admission for him to have to make. 3. Yes, and you're a nice son for a mother to have, aren't you? 4. A funny thing for a real gentleman like Mr Sleuth to do! 5. It was a terrifying fate for the three chums to contemplate. 6. Vivien is a hard name for an American boy to carry through life. 7. It wouldn't be right for a woman to see it. 8. His body was left in the Clock Tower for someone to discover in 1956. 9. How grand she had felt and how she had waved for everyone to see she was driving. 10. He nodded for the waiter to bring another bottle.

49 Translate, using *for* + infinitive group.

1. Im Tabakladen brannte auf der Theke ständig eine kleine Flamme, an der die Kunden ihre Zigaretten anzünden konnten. 2. Sie hatte die Terrine auf dem

Infinitive & -ing Form

Tisch gelassen, damit sich jeder selbst bedienen konnte. 3. Er brachte die Trophäe mit auf die Party, damit jeder sie bewundern konnte. 4. Sie nimmt das Baby mit, damit ihre Schwiegereltern es sich anschauen können. 5. Es ist an der Zeit, daß du ihm sagst, was du von seinen anrüchigen Geschäften hältst. 6. Ich glaube, es wird langsam Zeit, das Essen aufzutragen. 7. Am wichtigsten ist es für mich, daß ich ungestört malen kann. 8. Es steht uns nicht zu, an Gott zu zweifeln. 9. Das ist eine Sache, die Jack selbst entscheiden muß. 10. Das muß der Chef entscheiden. 11. Das müssen Ihre Fachleute entscheiden. 12. Es kommt gar nicht in Frage, daß du dich ihnen anschließt. 13. Es wäre unklug, wenn wir uns einmischten. 14. Es wäre sicherer, wenn du wartetest. 15. Jeder konnte deutlich sehen, daß er seine Arbeit haßte. 16. Es ist nicht gut, wenn sie da ganz allein draußen sitzt. 17. Es ist üblich, daß der Gefangene steht. 18. Es war keineswegs ungewöhnlich, daß Waren bar bezahlt wurden. 19. Es wird Zeit, daß du gehst. 20. Es ist für einen Untergebenen gefährlich, so eine Haltung einzunehmen.

50 Translate, using *for* + infinitive group.

1. Es gibt andere Gelegenheiten, bei denen sich ein Mann bewähren kann. 2. Es bleibt nichts mehr für uns zu tun. 3. Wir werden Rosen im Garten haben und Narzissen und einen Rasen, auf dem der kleine Billy und die kleine Barbara spielen können. 4. Ich möchte so gern, daß ihr beide euch kennenlernt. 5. Es dauerte sechs Wochen, bis mein Knöchel wieder in Ordnung war. 6. Es dauerte sechs Wochen, bis der Schnee geschmolzen war. 7. Es dauerte ungefähr eine Woche, bis mir dieser Gedanke kam. 8. Das Zimmer war gerade so groß, daß sich drei Menschen darin bewegen konnten. 9. Das Apollo-Raumschiff war so groß, daß ein Mann darin aufrecht stehen und umhergehen konnte. 10. Die einfachste Lösung war, daß er sofort nach London flog. 11. Es ist leichter, daß ein Kamel durch ein Nadelöhr geht als ein Reicher ins Himmelreich. 12. Er präsentierte sich in Hemdsärmeln, um sich von ihr die Krawatte geradeziehen zu lassen.

51 *With(out)* + (pro)noun + infinitive. – Sentences for observation and translation.

1. Edison took up this idea with the instantaneous camera and the celluloid film to help him.
2. With only ten days to go before the Premier arrives in Britain, our Government feels some dissatisfaction with the arrangements made for their stay.
3. I couldn't have coped with the work without someone to help me.
4. That's important for people without a place to live.
5. He will be kept busy with all this grass to cut.
6. Henceforth Britain would fight as a united country, with no party disputes to weaken her effort.

Infinitive & -ing Form

Translate, using the *with(out)* + (pro)noun + infinitive construction. **52**

1. Der Park würde sehr unsauber aussehen, wenn sich niemand darum kümmerte. 2. Wenn ein Mann nichts zu tun hat, langweilt er sich. 3. Die Frauen konnten nicht die ganze Arbeit in dem großen Haus machen und noch Essen für drei Kinder kochen, ohne daß ihnen jemand zur Hand ging. 4. Achtzehn Jahre lang durfte ich nicht die Treppe hinuntergehen, ohne daß mich jemand bei der Hand hielt. 5. Jetzt wo Flagler Pläne entwarf und Rockefeller ein wachsames Auge auf die Bücher, Arbeitsvorgänge und Angestellten hielt, machte die Firma bald Fortschritte. 6. Aber da mir nur noch eine Stunde blieb und ich noch packen und die Stadt durchqueren mußte, konnte ich meine Ungeduld nicht unterdrücken.

Sentences for observation. **53**

1. a) I am pleased to see you.
   b) I was pleased to see you.
   c) I shall be pleased to see you.
   d) I should be pleased to see you.
   e) I expect to see you tomorrow.
2. a) I am pleased to have seen you.
   b) I was pleased to have seen you.
   c) I shall be pleased to have seen you.
   d) I should be pleased to have seen you.
   e) I expect to have seen you by tomorrow night.

Translate the italicized forms in the following extract. Do you consider them as normal English or would you have expected different forms? If so, what forms? **54**

Hava: *I would like to have married* – a great man – a great singer – like someone I know.
Stone: *I would have liked to have been* a lawyer.
Segal: *I would have liked to have been* the leader of the greatest political party in the world . . .
Mrs Stone: *I would like to have been* a ballet dancer.
Bessie: *I would have liked to have married* a Rothschild.
White: *I would have liked to be* Joe Lyons.
Black: *I would have liked to have been* an Epstein . . .
Green: . . . *I would have liked to be* a Rabbi . . .
(From: Bernard Kops, *The Hamlet of Stepney Green*.)

Determine the meanings of the following sentences. **55**

1. a) I had hoped to see you.
   b) I hoped to have seen you.
   c) I had hoped to have seen you.

Infinitive & -ing Form

2. a) He is to play a part.
   b) He was to play a part.
   c) He was to have played a part.

56 Sentences for translation.

1. Er soll morgen kommen. 2. Er hätte gestern kommen sollen. 3. Du hättest ihrem Beispiel folgen sollen. 4. Ich wäre gerne gegangen. 5. Ich hatte gehofft, dich dort zu treffen. 6. Ich wollte eigentlich eine Woche dort bleiben. 7. Er sollte eigentlich gestern Wein kaufen. 8. Ich hatte beabsichtigt, den Brief schon vor einem Monat zu schreiben. 9. Du wärst besser bei uns geblieben. 10. Sie behauptete fälschlich, daß sie das Opfer von Drohungen gewesen sei. 11. Ihre Tochter hätte schon vor vielen Jahren heiraten sollen. 12. Es wäre doch besser für mich gewesen, eine Rückfahrkarte zu nehmen. 13. Ich hatte beabsichtigt, Ihnen heute morgen ein Trinkgeld zu geben. 14. Eine Gemäldeausstellung hätte eigentlich am 9. Juli im British Institute stattfinden sollen.

57 Sentences for observation and translation.

1. a) *Being English*, she set a higher value on material possessions than did Dr Brennan.
   b) *Not having any fancy ideas or much money*, I decided to go to the pictures.
   c) *Returning from the station*, he passed a cinema.
   d) *Coming out of the hotel*, he made straight for the nearest bookstore.
   e) *Puffing on an English cigarette*, he retreated behind a wall of silence.
   f) *Undressing slowly*, he got into bed.
   g) *Opening her bag*, she took out a packet of cigarettes.
2. a) Their agent was killed last night in Finland, *travelling under another name*.
   b) He was standing in front of the mirror, *shaving with an electric razor*.
   c) Stewart paid the driver and got out of the taxi, *looking at his watch*.
   d) She had entered the room, *hoping her nervousness wouldn't show*.
   e) He was dangerous, *being clever and patient*.
3. a) The girl, *laughing*, moved away.
   b) John, *feeling a little better*, came down to lunch.
   c) The wind, *blowing through the trees*, made a whistling sound.
   d) Mrs Albemarle, *realizing the danger*, intervened.
4. a) The man *pacing the floor* is Mr Barish.
   b) The girl *sitting over there* is Maggie Hoskins.
   c) This morning I got a note from my aunt *asking me to come for lunch*.
   d) His eyes began to gleam like those of a cat *scenting a plump mouse*.

58 Sentences for translation.

1. Die Greens saßen um den Küchentisch und aßen ihr Abendbrot. 2. Einen Augenblick lang saßen sie da und schauten sich an. 3. Er legte die Zeitung hin

Infinitive & -ing Form

und ging in die Küche. 4. Er ging in sein Zimmer zurück und setzte sich an seinen Schreibtisch, um einen Brief zu schreiben. 5. Ich griff zum Telefon und meldete den Anruf der Polizei. 6. Ich ging ins Zimmer und schloß die Tür hinter mir. 7. Als ich meinen Kaffee getrunken hatte, ging ich zum Schreibtisch. 8. Nachdem sie sich abgetrocknet hatte, kämmte sie sich schnell die Haare und schaute fragend in den Spiegel. 9. Als ich auf die Uhr schaute, sah ich, daß es zehn Uhr war. 10. Während ich die Straße am Marble Arch überquerte, sah ich jemanden, den ich von Paris her kannte. 11. Da sie erst siebzehn war, durfte sie in Wirtschaften noch nicht hinein. 12. Da ich sah, daß die Füße des Kindes naß waren, machte ich ein Feuer und zog ihm die Schuhe aus. 13. So schnell ich konnte, raste ich zur Garage, wo sich mir ein schrecklicher Anblick bot. 14. Äußerlich blieb sie ruhig und verließ selten die Abgeschiedenheit ihrer Wohnung. 15. Das kleine Mädchen, das sich vor der Dunkelheit fürchtete, ließ die ganze Nacht über das Licht brennen. 16. Er war von schlankem Wuchs und hatte eine frische Gesichtsfarbe; deshalb sah er viel jünger aus als Herr Jones. 17. Er kroch den Hügel hinauf, wobei er sich auf Ellbogen und Händen vorwärts schleppte und den Koffer vor sich herschob. 18. Sie verschloß die Tür, machte die Lampen an und öffnete das Fenster. 19. Er spannte einen Bogen Papier in seine Schreibmaschine, zündete sich eine Zigarette an und tippte wütend drauflos. 20. Ich nahm den Hörer auf, hielt ihn ans Ohr und sagte: „Hallo!"

Use *-ing* constructions instead of the relative clauses in the following sentences. Say in which cases the *-ing* construction is not permissible. | **59**

1. She called good night to those girls who were not going in her direction. 2. His hair, which was beginning to grey, was trimmed in a perpetual crew cut. 3. The plumber who repaired our sink has sent his bill. 4. They sat inside the big plexiglass dome like goldfish that were expecting food. 5. On the wall were a couple of well-framed military prints of soldiers in red coats and shakos who were sitting on horses. 6. I showed him the table that needed a coat of paint. 7. The teacher admonished the boys who were laughing. 8. What is the name of the boy who brought us the letter? 9. For anyone who attempts to discuss a book about murders, some acquaintance with De Quincey's essay is necessary. 10. A police constable who was walking his beat near Waterloo Road at about two in the morning witnessed the not unusual sight of a man being let out of a house by a young girl. 11. The men who had been setting up the safe came downstairs spitting on their hands and rubbing them on their jeans. 12. The street lamp over the way vaguely disclosed the vacuum cleaners which were standing around like tombs. 13. He felt the sad relief of a man who realizes that there is one love at least that no longer hurts him. 14. Peering through a dusty glass pane, I saw a dimly-lit room which looked as though it had not been occupied for a long time.

Infinitive & -ing Form

60 Combine the following pairs of sentences, using -ing.

1. He spoke slowly. He carefully articulated each syllable. 2. His eyes were grey and moved slowly. They took in his surroundings with care and awe. 3. I approached him from behind. Then I touched him on the arm. 4. He lit his cigarette. He took a gulp of the acrid smoke and turned to face the landlady as she ran into the room. 5. I wanted to write better on birds and bird diseases. Therefore I took a course in English syntax. 6. The doctor appeared, bag in hand. He was wearing an overcoat over his pyjamas. 7. I opened the first-aid kit. Then I bandaged my injured hand. 8. I tried to pass the time. So I leafed through a few magazines. 9. I was feeling restless. Therefore I went out to put the car in the garage. 10. She had altered her position. As a result she could now see both sides of the stranger's face. 11. I've written to my uncle. I've asked him to let me know when he's coming. 12. He put on a clean shirt as fast as he could. Then he hurried to the office. 13. They are women. Consequently they are of rather more conservative temperament than ourselves. 14. The threatening clouds had passed by. They had left the air hot and still over the city. 15. I sat on the edge of my bed. I watched Jenny unpack the few things we had brought.

61 Sentences for observation and translation.

1. a) He was adding to the confusion *by asking me questions*.
   b) "I'm sorry," Skip said, "*for not having sherry*."
   c) She managed to let me play at being the boss *without being obsequious about it*.
   d) *Besides driving and looking after the car*, he took care of the garden.
   e) *On hearing this news*, he decided to leave immediately.
   f) *In choosing our dress*, we must not forget the quality of the material.
   g) *Instead of apologizing*, he hurried away without a word.
2. a) I sat down in one of the large chairs and began, *while looking official*, thinking of dates at random and trying to remember what had happened.
   b) He paused for a long time *as though thinking carefully* before he answered my question.
   c) *After graduating* she took a trip round the world with her grandfather.
   d) When he came out of prison he worked briefly for a firm of cleaners *before being sacked for dishonesty*.
   e) *When coming home from the office* he noticed that something was wrong.
   f) He was not the equal of Lloyd George in attack *though excelling him in such speeches*.

62 Sentences for translation.

1. Der Einbrecher entkam in der Dunkelheit, ohne daß man ihn erkannte. 2. Nachdem ich meinen Kaffee ausgetrunken hatte, setzte ich mich an meinen Schreibtisch.

3. Während ich im Hyde Park einem Redner zuhörte, gewahrte ich plötzlich jemand, den ich von der Hochschule her kannte. 4. Er lächelte, und dabei rieb er mit dem Stiel seiner Pfeife an seinem Schnurrbart. 5. Nachdem sie sich abgetrocknet hatte, kämmte sie sich schnell das Haar und schaute fragend in den Spiegel. 6. Als sie aus dem Haus traten, sahen sie den Mann, der ihnen vom Bahnhof her gefolgt war. 7. Abgesehen davon, daß er Vorräte bestellen mußte, bestand seine einzige Aufgabe darin, an der Bar zu stehen und wie ein Gentleman auszusehen. 8. Als ich mich mit ihnen stritt, fühlte ich mich plötzlich schuldig, weil mir das Streiten Spaß machte. 9. Nachdem wir Trinidad besucht hatten, wollten wir unbedingt auch Martinique sehen. 10. Sie schlief zehn Stunden, ohne sich zu rühren. 11. Wir wissen beide, daß wir unseren Kragen riskieren, wenn wir nicht vorsichtig mit unseren Aussagen sind. 12. Wir vertrieben uns die Zeit mit Kartenspielen. 13. Du solltest ihn nicht kritisieren, weil er ein Nationalist ist. 14. Als er nach London kam, arbeitete er für kurze Zeit bei einer Presseagentur, bevor er sich als freiberuflicher Journalist etablierte. 15. Venedig versuchte, den Verlust dieses Handelszweiges dadurch wettzumachen, daß es mit Ägypten und Arabien Handel trieb. 16. Durch das sorgfältige Studium dieses Buches kann man viel lernen. 17. Jeder Mann des ersten Zuges wurde bei dem Versuch, die Brücke zu überqueren, verwundet. 18. Sobald Davies von diesem Versuch erfahren hatte, verflüssigte er ein anderes Gas auf dieselbe Art. 19. Er dachte an die geringe Summe, die ihm übriggeblieben war, nachdem er die Rechnung bezahlt hatte. 20. Sie trat vor und hob die Hand, als wolle sie zwischen die beiden Streitenden treten.

Misrelated *-ing*. – Put the following sentences right. | 63 |

1. One day when out working the branch of a tree fell across his back, pinning him to the ground. 2. Being rather withdrawn by nature, it had presented no difficulty to him to preserve the distance that he thought prudent. 3. Viewing the whole evidence, death could not be attributed to acute dysentery. 4. Arriving at a great mass meeting in Essex, a brick smashed through the window of their car, narrowly missing injuring them both. 5. Staggering to our feet, overcome with despair, the stony ice slope seemed quite unnegotiable. 6. While driving home from his midnight broadcast through the Green Forest, a figure had hailed him. 7. Walking to school today, my arithmetic book fell in the gutter. 8. Having opened his eyes so suddenly, seeing nothing but the sky and the horizon, Rodney's mind was empty. 9. The maid thought that he was already dead, but on pouring some water from the carafe over his forehead he opened his eyes. 10. Upon dying I succeeded to his property.

Sentences for observation and translation. | 64 |

1. a) *Staying behind* is dangerous.
   b) *You / Your staying behind* is dangerous.
2. a) The difficulty was *having to convince him.*
   b) The difficulty was *me / my having to convince him.*

Infinitive & -ing Form

   3. a) I hate *having to lie about it.*
      b) I hate *the children / the children's having to lie about it.*
   4. a) They insisted on *consulting a specialist.*
      b) They insisted on *the doctor / the doctor's consulting a specialist.*

65 In which of the following sentences can the object case be replaced by the possessive?

1. His father had insisted on *Carswell* going into the regiment. 2. Dalby hated *me* concentrating. 3. He just couldn't bear the thought of *a sergeant* rubbing shoulders with him at the Mirabelle. 4. The handing-over ceremony consisted of *Tony and Alice* showing me how to work the IBM. 5. Although we had no trace of *him* visiting or phoning Tatsfield where Maclean lived, they did cross paths. 6. The back-benchers insisted on *the treaty* being ratified. 7. *You* being so quiet in the lift was what I appreciated. 8. Fancy *a woman of taste* buying a hat like that! 9. I can't imagine *his daughter* marrying so young. 10. What's the use of *him* coming? 11. I hate the idea of *you* wasting your time. 12. I'm not ashamed of *my father* being poor. 13. I don't doubt you're right about *him* being a socialist at heart. 14. We were surprised at *Anne* inviting us to her party. 15. They were executed without *either of them* having made a confession.

66 Sentences for translation.

1. Ich gab das Schreiben Tom, der es vorlas, ohne daß sich sein Gesichtsausdruck dabei veränderte. 2. Es bestand die Gefahr, daß der Schmuck gestohlen wurde. 3. Daß unsere Gegner das glauben, überrascht mich nicht. 4. Er muß die Möglichkeit berücksichtigt haben, daß wir dabei erwischt werden könnten. 5. Die Krankenschwester bestand darauf, daß der Arzt wieder geholt wurde. 6. Wir wollen verhindern, daß es noch einmal passiert. 7. Du solltest dich sehr geehrt fühlen, daß du und Richard die einzigen Herren sind, die die Damen begleiten dürfen. 8. Ich bin sehr erstaunt darüber, daß du diese Frage mit ihm besprochen hast. 9. Der Umstand, daß ich schwach bin, gibt dir nicht das Recht, mich zu beleidigen. 10. Ich habe wirklich was dagegen, daß dieser junge Bengel raucht. 11. Als die Tür geöffnet wurde, sah ich zunächst gar nichts. 12. Der Erfolg der ganzen Sache hängt davon ab, daß sich jeder streng an den Plan hält. 13. Er zweifelte nicht daran, daß es höchst angenehm für Fanny war. 14. Der Arzt hat nichts dagegen, daß ich hin und wieder ein Stückchen Fleisch esse. 15. Was nützt es eigentlich, daß ich mit so einem Dummkopf rede? 16. Es hat gar keinen Zweck, daß du dauernd hier herumlungerst. 17. Daß mein Freund sie begleitete, war für sie ein großer Vorteil. 18. Als man ihm etwas Schnaps verabreichte, kam er wieder zu sich. 19. Kann ich mich darauf verlassen, daß ihr alle den Mund haltet?

Infinitive & -ing Form

67 Translate, using the verbs in brackets.

1. Er verdient es, daß man ihm hilft. (deserve) 2. Die Theorie ist einer Betrachtung wert. (deserve) 3. Sie müssen einen Arzt aufsuchen. (need) 4. Dieses Kapitel muß neu geschrieben werden. (need) 5. Das bedarf einer Erklärung. (need) 6. Die Kanadier bedürfen nicht der Befreiung. (need) 7. Er will sofort benachrichtigt werden. (want) 8. Das Badezimmer muß gestrichen werden. (want) 9. Das Kind muß dauernd beaufsichtigt werden. (want) 10. Wollen Sie zu einer bestimmten Zeit geweckt werden? (want) 11. Mein Wagen muß repariert werden. (want) 12. Der Aufsatz muß überarbeitet werden. (require) 13. Er ist nicht mehr zu retten. (be past) 14. Das Buch ist es nicht wert, gelesen zu werden. (be worth) 15. Das Ergebnis ist nicht der Rede wert. (be worth) 16. Seine Worte lassen sich unmöglich wiederholen. (not to bear)

68 The absolute *-ing* construction. – Sentences for observation and translation.

1. When I returned home, I found the house empty, *my mother being at the shops.*
2. At three o'clock the men from the Cleansing Department came to empty the dustbin, *Monday being the day on which this was usually done.*
3. It had happened just as they were ready to go, *the car waiting in the road, promising views of the sea and hills.*
4. They took the bus to Hyde Park Corner, *Blythe paying the fares,* and then walked to a large house.
5. *The value of x being known,* the value of y can be found.
6. Again we exchanged offers, *with neither side taking up the option.*
7. Most dairy products are imported, *with the home industry only producing about a quarter.*
8. "This is just a sample selection, *with more coming along every day,*" said the institute.
9. This would permit a diminished State sector to operate more efficiently *with purpose-built comprehensive schools being developed in those areas where they are required.*
10. Less than half a second covered the first five, *with Betty Jenkins taking second place ahead of Shirley Benton.*

69 Combine the following sentences, using the absolute *-ing* construction.

1. Today, Texas accents give the orders at Southampton, and the staff strength is back to about sixty. 2. Party strategists clearly think that the best form of defence is attack. The assault should be directed at Labour Ministers. 3. She tapped on the wall of his hut when she was ready, for she was better at waking up in the morning than he. 4. The lavatory was whitewashed every year. Either he or Harry gave it a new coat in the spring. 5. "Twenty kilos," Dalby said. His thin lips formed the words yet again in tacit joy. 6. Each is playing his own

Infinitive & -ing Form

game, but Britain as usual plays her game a damn sight less effectively than the others. 7. I saw him throwing his head back. His long hair flashed in the hot sunshine. 8. It was early-closing day in the town where she worked as a waitress. That's why she was home early. 9. William Kellogg pushed forward to the bench. Tears were coursing down his face. 10. In Devon, the A9 between Barnstaple and Bridgwater was very difficult. The notoriously steep Porlock Hill was impassable and single-line traffic operated in other places. 11. "I'd be most interested to hear it," he said. His small bright eyes were looking over the menu carefully. 12. Sitting on his dressing-room bench, Ellis turned his slightly prominent eyes on me. Sweat was running out of his hair. 13. He had three children. The youngest was the same age as Dorothy. 14. The bus was very crowded. So John had to stand. 15. I always endeavour to speak of Sir Thomas with the greatest respect, for he is a magistrate and a Member of Parliament.

70 Sentences for observation and translation.

1. *Having* a relationship with an artist is a different kettle of fish from *having* a relationship with an ordinary man.
2. *Being* here makes me feel all over again what a marvellous thing our friendship is.
3. Father *travelling* to London has got nothing to do with it.
4. There was much *clearing* of throats and *coughing*.
5. There was no *mistaking* the relief in Bill's voice.
6. Suddenly it was quite useless *attempting* to pray.
7. It's no use *blinding* yourself to the facts.
8. There's no use in both Eileen and me *losing* you.
9. My chief occupations were *reading* and *writing*.
10. I don't think it queer your *giving* him the money, but it's queer your never *mentioning* it.
11. I just thought that you were the sort worth *sticking* by.
12. It's an awful responsibility *being* alone at such a time.
13. On Thursday I was busy *working* over a backlog of new information.
14. You can't prevent *looting* until you have police there in sufficient numbers.
15. My complaint about *working* in the dark must have had some effect.
16. He brought 20 kilos of heroin across from Syria within seven days of *getting* his licence.
17. She hardly dared breathe for fear of *disturbing* him and *making* him angry.
18. Conference leaders discouraged delegates from *talking* to reporters.
19. You didn't waste much time in *having* me brought to justice, did you?
20. It was all very close to *being* a miracle.
21. The Socialists were not alone in *expressing* their indignation.
22. He'd better devote all his energy to *apologizing*.
23. I don't feel like *swimming* today.

Infinitive & -ing Form

24. Are any of the traditional problems of philosophy any nearer to *being* solved by us than they were by the Greeks?
25. Bill was a long time *answering*.
26. We were late *getting* here.
27. He took his time *lighting* a cigarette.
28. A dirty child with torn trousers and a pair of American canvas shoes drove three goats *clattering* along the road to the north.
29. The sight through the window of the point of a blue helmet had me *moving* back up the stairs again.
30. The many large commercial concerns which have industrial espionage teams *spying* on competitors must submit monthly reports.
31. They found him *fishing* for trout.
32. I caught him *opening* my letters.
33. He didn't think the British public would veto entry as *being* too costly.

Translate, using *-ing*. | 71 |

1. Wenn man dir so zuhört, bekommt man wieder Hoffnung. 2. Fliegen ist die angenehmste Art des Reisens. 3. Wenn man den ganzen Nachmittag in der Stadt herumschlendert, wird man ziemlich durstig. 4. Die Befolgung äußerlicher Regeln ist nicht das höchste ethische Ideal. 5. Über Geschmack läßt sich nicht streiten. 6. Wenn er in Wut gerät, kann man ihn einfach nicht mehr halten. 7. Man kann nicht wissen, was er in einer solchen Situation tut. 8. Für einen ungelernten Arbeiter war da nichts zu machen. 9. Bis spät in die Nacht wurde gesungen und gelacht. 10. Aus dir ist keine direkte Antwort auf irgendeine Frage herauszuholen. 11. Ich habe noch nichts angerührt, seit ich das Haus verlassen habe. – Dann ist es doch ganz lächerlich, daß du nichts ißt. 12. Es ist herrlich, die Frau eines Künstlers zu sein. 13. Es war wunderbar, daß er an einem Sonntag kam. 14. Es ist absolut zwecklos, irgend etwas zu besprechen. 15. Es dauert ein wenig, bis man sich an sie gewöhnt hat. 16. Ich bin es nicht gewohnt, daß man an meinen Worten zweifelt. 17. Hast du dich darum gekümmert, daß das ganze Gepäck richtig verstaut worden ist? 18. Für die Lösung dieses Problems gibt es keine unüberwindlichen Schwierigkeiten. 19. Ich bin einfach nicht dazu gekommen, dich zu fragen, während sie hier war. 20. Ich freue mich darauf, am Wochenende nach Paris zu fahren. 21. Wie alle dicken Leute gab er nie zu, daß er dick war. 22. Die ganze Zeit über träumte ich davon, eines Tages ein großer Maler zu werden. 23. Ich bin ein wenig betrübt, wenn ich daran denke, daß meine Frau mich verläßt. 24. Wir beglückwünschten ihn, daß er die Angelegenheit zufriedenstellend geregelt hatte. 25. Ich bestehe darauf, daß du heute abend hierbleibst. 26. Wenn er einmal zu der Ansicht gekommen ist, daß etwas richtig ist, kann ihn keine Macht der Welt davon abbringen, es zu tun. 27. Ich kann deinem Vater keine Vorwürfe machen wegen seines Wunsches, daß du sie heiratest. 28. Der Streit endete damit, daß Romeo nach Mantua verbannt wurde. 29. Die meiste Zeit verbrachte er mit Lesen und Schlafen. 30. Betty überredete mich dazu, ihr das Kleid zu kaufen.

Infinitive & -ing Form

72 Translate, using *-ing*.

1. Ich wundere mich darüber, daß du kommst und mir Moralpredigten über Liebe und Ehe hältst. 2. Sie zog eine Schürze an und ging daran, das Abendessen vorzubereiten. 3. Ich mußte noch viel darüber lernen, wie man mit Menschen umging. 4. Ich würde nicht das Geringste dagegen einwenden, daß du ihn heiratest. 5. Er ging nach England in der Absicht, in London ein Geschäft zu eröffnen. 6. Er war erfreut, daß er mit einem Mann im Dorf ein gutes Geschäft gemacht hatte. 7. Ich bin überrascht, daß du und dieser scheußliche Kerl so dicke Freunde seid. 8. Sie war drauf und dran, Selbstmord zu begehen. 9. Ich hatte nicht die geringste Absicht, dich zu beleidigen. 10. Im Augenblick hat die Polizei keinen Grund, irgend jemanden zu verdächtigen. 11. Welchen Grund hast du, all diese Lügen über mich zu verbreiten? 12. Es liegt mir fern, dich zu kritisieren. 13. Es ist Unsinn, daß wir uns streiten. 14. Es dauerte nicht lange, bis die Antwort kam. 15. Ich hatte keine Lust, diese Frage zu beantworten.

73 Translate, using *-ing*.

1. „Er liebt mich nicht", jammerte sie, und ihre Tränen nahmen zu. 2. Einen Augenblick lang lag Maria in seinen Armen, und ihr Herz schlug so schnell wie das eines Vogels. 3. Die Konventionen sind ebenso bindend wie die Regeln eines Spiels, denn ohne Regeln ist kein Spiel möglich. 4. Er sagte, daß der Minister neben der Gräfin X sitzen müsse, denn sie sei doch der wichtigste Gast. 5. Da im Hause für mich kein Platz war, suchte ich mir ein Zimmer in einem Gasthaus. 6. „Ich weiß", sagte sie mit zitternder Stimme. 7. Mit klopfendem Herzen sah Mary mir zu, wie ich den Brief öffnete. 8. Es ist wirklich reizend, daß wir euch alle hier haben. Und da James heute abend auch noch herüberkommt, wird es eine richtige Familienversammlung. 9. Jetzt wo dein Mann doch alles weiß, kann ich nicht länger hierbleiben. 10. Es war so düster, und der Regen prasselte den ganzen Tag auf die Fenster. 11. Jetzt wo beide Jungen arbeitslos sind und der Vater im Sterben liegt, weiß ich einfach nicht, was man für diese Unglücklichen tun kann.

74 Translate, using *-ing*.

1. Du kannst es doch nicht zulassen, daß er sich so benimmt. 2. Ich habe mehrere Probleme, die mir Kopfzerbrechen machen. 3. Eine Dame kommt heute Nachmittag zum Tee zu mir. 4. In ein paar Monaten hat er uns soweit, daß wir Englisch sprechen können. 5. Wir werden die Dinge bald in Gang bringen. 6. Ich fand mich plötzlich dem großen Manne gegenüber. 7. Wir fanden ihn bei der Arbeit an seinem Schreibtisch. 8. Obwohl der Premierminister voller Optimismus sprach, ließ er seine Zuhörer darüber im unklaren, was die Zukunft bringen würde. 9. Laß mich dich nicht noch einmal dabei erwischen! 10. Ich erwischte ihn, als er in meinem Garten Äpfel stahl. 11. Laß den Motor anspringen. 12. Er

Infinitive & -ing Form

setzte die Maschine in Gang. 13. Sie ließen mich draußen stehen. 14. Erwähnen Sie nicht, daß ich so etwas vorgeschlagen habe. 15. Es fällt mir doch auf, daß sie ein reizendes Mädchen ist.

The Tenses

75 The simple present. – Sentences for observation.

1. a) Business lunches *stretch* out endlessly.
   b) For some people the country *signifies* peace.
   c) The early bird *catches* the worm.
2. a) I usually *wear* a coat.
   b) How *do* you *play* this game?
   c) He *works* very hard and *publishes* a book every year.
3. a) You're sacked, he said, you *leave* at the end of the week.
   b) Your subscription *expires* on the 16th inst.
   c) The trunks are packed; we *start* tomorrow.
4. a) I'll telephone you when he *comes*.
   b) I guess you owe me something, and as soon as I'*m* fit again, I'll collect.
5. a) If the weather *is* fine tomorrow, we shall have a picnic.
   b) If I *catch* you at it again, you'll get a sound beating.
6. a) The Conqueror succeeded to all the rights of the old kings, but his council now *is* mainly French-born and French-speaking. The tendency to provincialization *is* arrested; the king's peace *is* everywhere ...
   b) (*Of past events:*) She *turns* on the light, the murderers *seize* her, she *struggles* and *yells* for help.
7. a) Here *comes* the bride.
   b) There *goes* my bus.
   c) Up *goes* the flag.
8. a) I *see* your point.
   b) The headmaster *wants* to speak to you.
   c) "It's filthy outside." – "I *don't mind* the weather."
9. a) He *comes* fairly close and they *stare* at each other.
   b) He *stirs* the fire, *trims* the lamp, *arranges* some books and papers, *sits* down, *is* restless, *shivers* slightly, the clock *strikes* twelve, and he *settles* to read.
10. a) I *wish* I was home.
    b) I *wish* I could trust you.
    c) I *wish* we had known the truth.

76 Translate the following sentences into German, noting the difference in tense.

1. I *understand* there was a disturbance. 2. We *understand* you only arrived yesterday. 3. I *hear* you've bought a house. 4. I *see* in the papers that the King is ill. 5. I *find* among my letters a note concerning you. 6. I saw him once, but I *forget* where it was.

77 Explain the use of the progressive forms in the following passage.

Mummy and Daddy *are coming*. They'*re coming* past the shrimping pools, they'*re climbing* up the shingle. – Now Daddy *is waving*, now Mummy *is wav-*

The Tenses

ing. Now they're in the sand dunes. Mummy *is slipping*, and Daddy *is pulling* her up. Now they*'re coming*.

Compare the passage in **77** with the following passages. | **78**

1. (Stage direction:) A frail old man *levers* himself up from his lying position in the bed; it is Sam and he *wears* pyjamas; he looks around.
2. (Stage direction:) The front door *opens* and Nicky *comes* in. He is Gillian's brother, a little younger, and has an engaging, impish and somewhat impertinent personality. He *wears* a dinner jacket, topcoat, and *carries* some small Christmas-wrapped packages.
3. (Announcer introducing radio play:) It is an afternoon in winter. The living room of the Carters' house is a shambles. Carter *is sitting* at the table, picking at the crumbs on the newspaper tablecloth. Waxman *enters*. He *looks* at Carter. Carter *ignores* him. Slowly Waxman *removes* his overcoat. He *looks* at Carter again, but getting no response, *clears* a pile of newspapers from the couch and *sits*.

Note the use of the simple form in the following examples. | **79**

1. (Conjurer:) Ladies and gentlemen, you see I *take* a coin; I *place* it here on the table; I *cover* it with the glass.
2. (Sports reporter on radio:) He *catches* the ball, he *drops* it, he *picks* it up again, he *runs* forward with it . . .
3. (Cookery demonstration:) I *take* three eggs and *beat* them in this basin. Then I *add* sugar . . .
4. (Salesman demonstrating vacuum cleaner:) You see how it *sucks* up the dust.

What is the difference between the simple form and the progressive form in each of the following pairs of sentences? | **80**

1. a) He *limps*.
   b) He *is limping*.
2. a) What *does* he *do*?
   b) What *is* he *doing*?
3. a) The bucket *leaks*.
   b) The bucket *is leaking*.
4. a) I think you're very cruel.
   b) I think you're *being* very cruel.
5. a) She's a hysterical old woman.
   b) She's *being* a hysterical old woman.
6. a) He *goes* to work by bus.
   b) He's *going* to work by bus.

The Tenses

7. a) What *do* you *think*?
   b) What *are* you *thinking*?
8. a) *Do* you *feel* all right this morning?
   b) *Are* you *feeling* all right this morning?
9. a) She *looks* very pretty.
   b) She*'s looking* very pretty.
10. a) If you*'re telling* me the truth, you have nothing to fear.
    b) If you *tell* me the truth, you have nothing to fear.
11. a) Whenever I see him, he *runs* away.
    b) Whenever I see him, he*'s running* away.
12. a) He always *comes* to see me.
    b) He's always *coming* to see me.
13. a) *Do* they *speak* English?
    b) *Are* they *speaking* English?
14. a) Why *do* you *use* a knife for that?
    b) Why on earth *are* you *using* a knife for that?
15. a) The statue *stands* in the market place.
    b) The statue *is* still *standing* in the market place.
16. a) Now she *sings* beautifully.
    b) Now she *is singing* beautifully.
17. a) Look, it *floats*.
    b) Look, it *is floating*.
18. a) I *start* work next Monday.
    b) I*'m starting* work next Monday.

81 Study the following sentences. Would the simple form be equally correct?

1. Don't let's appear to *be holding* a conference.
2. She*'s getting* very deaf, isn't she?
3. Gill, what the hell *are* you *getting* at?
4. "We*'re winning* the war," the general answered confidently.
5. This young couple whose room you*'re having* had an old aunt here years and years, till she was carried off with a stroke.

82 Choose the most natural forms.

1. Tobacco (becomes, is becoming) the vice of my middle age. 2. I hope (I don't disturb, I'm not disturbing) you too much. 3. Martin, darling, don't pretend to be a cynic and not to care – it just (doesn't ring, isn't ringing) true. 4. The house (faces, is facing) south. 5. You can't miss the church; its spire (towers, is towering) above the other buildings round about. 6. My sister (has, is having) some of her friends in for tea, and they're chattering like a hundred canaries.

The Tenses

Comment on the use of the progressive form in the following sentences. **83**

1. Mother, I'*m being* serious. In about a month from now I'm going to get myself a job.
2. You'*re being* strangely generous with him.
3. Oh, don't be silly, Howard! – I'*m* not *being* silly.
4. "You'*re* not *being* nice, are you?" – "I'*m* not *being* intentionally unpleasant," he answered quickly.
5. You'*re being* ridiculous.
6. I'm extremely grateful to you for being so rational about it. – I'*m* not *being* rational.
7. Miss Bradley had an accident. She was killed in a fall and the police *are being* very difficult.

Study the following sentences. What attitude on the part of the speaker is suggested? Translate the sentences into German. **84**

1. Why *are* you always *picking* on me?
2. He *is* continually *contradicting* me.
3. She'*s* always *gadding* about and *gossiping* with the neighbours.
4. I'*m* for ever *making* such stupid mistakes.
5. He's always *grumbling*.
6. She's always *asking* silly questions.
7. In New York they'*re* always *tearing* up the pavement.
8. I'*m* continually *losing* my spectacles.

Sentences for translation. **85**

1. Das Kind schreit aber auch immer. 2. Er läßt aber auch immer alles fallen. 3. Verflixt, ich vergesse doch immer alles. 4. Ich nehme immer den 9-Uhr-Zug. 5. Das verdammte Auto geht aber auch immer kaputt. 6. Immer wenn ich nach Hause fahren will, geht das Auto kaputt. 7. In Köln werden aber auch dauernd die Straßen aufgerissen. 8. Er kommt immer bei uns zu Besuch, wenn er in London ist. 9. Er redet fortwährend von Ehrlichkeit, als ob er der einzige ehrliche Mensch wäre. 10. Wenn ich Kuchen backe, dann schlage ich immer zuerst die Eier auf.

Comment on the use or non-use of the progressive form in the following sentences. **86**

1. a) I *smell* flowers.
   b) The flowers *smell* lovely.
   c) The girl *is smelling* the flowers.
2. a) I *taste* salt in the soup.
   b) The soup *tastes* salty.

The Tenses

    c) The cook *is tasting* the soup.
3. a) I *feel* something rough.
    b) The cloth *feels* rough.
    c) I'*m feeling* the cloth to see if it's rough.

87   Sentences for translation.

1. Die Pferde riechen das Wasser schon aus drei Kilometern Entfernung. 2. Der Hund beriecht den Laternenpfahl. 3. Katinka riecht nach Knoblauch. 4. Die Köchin riecht an dem Fisch, um festzustellen, ob man ihn noch essen kann. 5. Was machst du da? – Ich schmecke die Soße ab, um herauszufinden, ob ich Salz oder Zucker drangetan habe. Aber ich muß sagen, sie schmeckt gut. 6. Sie fühlt, ob der Stoff reine Seide ist oder nicht. Er fühlt sich mehr wie Kunstseide an. 7. Ich rieche an dem Brief, um festzustellen, ob sie parfümiertes Briefpapier benutzt.

88   Why is the progressive form used in the following sentences?

1. It's one of the few days of the year when the town *isn't smelling* like the inside of an old garage.
2. My usual cigarettes *are tasting* a bit flat.

89   What does the progressive form signal in the following sentences?

1. a) He'*s going* to work by bus.
    b) We'*re eating* a lot more meat now.
    c) We'*re eating* supper out this week.
2. a) They'*re visiting* us more and more often.
    b) He'*s looking* more and more like his father.
    c) The subject of intonation *is receiving* more and more attention.

90   Study the following examples. In which of them would the simple form be a) better, b) equally good, or c) impossible? In cases where both forms are equally good, can you detect any difference in meaning?

1. Can I *be giving* you a hand, Mrs Fisher?
2. I'll look after Mr Sleuth. He may *be wanting* his supper just a bit earlier than usual today.
3. The kettle must *be boiling* by now.
4. I really must *be going*.
5. "Here, have a cigarette," she said. "You must *be needing* one."
6. "Yes, you mustn't *be forgetting* the lodger's supper," called out Bunting.
7. Why *are* you *having* to do it on the sly, anyhow?
8. I'*m needing* the money, I tell you.
9. "Now Father, Father dear," said Mrs Parker, "don't *be taking* any notice of him, he's up in the air today with the promise of £500 from Mr Balintore."

The Tenses

91 Simple or progressive form? – Make any necessary adjustments in word order.

1. You (think) the children (miss) their mother?
2. I hope I (not keep) you from your supper.
3. She (go) to the pictures twice a week.
4. You (help) me out of a tight corner, darling. You (be) an angel.
5. I say, Georgie, you (look) terribly smart today. Quite the up-to-date girl.
6. I need your advice. I (plan) my holidays, you know.
7. Nowadays they (be) scientific. They (spray) the locusts and (kill) miles and miles of them. They (fly) up in aeroplanes and (aim) poison at them.
8. I only (taste) the soup. I'm not going to eat it.
9. They are notoriously incompetent payers of their men. Their centres constantly (run) out of funds.
10. David, try and be a good guy for a change. Your father (die).
11. Nothing, she answered in a small voice, I (be) just silly.
12. Christmas (come) but once a year.
13. Here the teacher (come).
14. I (forget) names nowadays.
15. What you (do)? I mean what's your job?
16. You (listen) to what I (tell) you?
17. No wine for me, please. It (taste) sour.
18. You (plan) to get married?
19. He for ever (snub) friendly advances.
20. Observe, ladies and gentlemen, I (put) the card in the hat.
21. In Britain, history and ancient pageantry (live) side by side with trends, styles and fashions that (delight) the modern world.
22. Terry (stand) up and (walk) round the end of the bed towards the bedroom door and Jess. Terry (wear) a nightdress. Jess (wear) a dressing gown over pyjamas ... Terry (touch) Jess lightly on the shoulder as she (walk) past her and (smile). Terry (walk) across the hall to the bathroom door and (go) in. The transistor radio (stand) on the edge of the bath. Terry (walk) along the side of the bath and (bend) to pick it up. As she (straighten) up again, the room (spin) and Terry (lurch) sideways, reaching for the wall ... She (shake) her head abruptly and (push) away from the wall, turning towards the door. Jess (stand) in the doorway.

92 Miscellaneous sentences for translation.

1. Das war so, Herr Richter. Ich sitze ganz ruhig da und kümmere mich um meinen eigenen Kram, als ich plötzlich von hinten eins auf die Birne bekomme. 2. Er hat Fieber. 3. Du benimmst dich wieder mal wie ein Kind. 4. Gestern habe ich mich nicht sehr wohl gefühlt, aber heute fühle ich mich besser. 5. Ich habe das Gefühl, es wird ein toller Erfolg. 6. Du gähnst? Ich langweile dich doch nicht etwa? 7. Er weiß, wovon er redet. 8. Das Leben wird immer teurer. 9. Warum hat es mit unserer Ehe nicht geklappt? Was ist aus unserer Liebe ge-

The Tenses

worden? Oh, ich mache dir keinen Vorwurf. Ich frage dich bloß. 10. Wie geht es Lottie? – Sehr gut. Sie wohnt jetzt in Hamburg. 11. Immer mehr Leute kaufen Fernsehgeräte. 12. Das spielt jetzt immer weniger eine Rolle. 13. Wir frühstücken immer um 9 Uhr. 14. Wir stehen diese Woche früher auf als sonst. 15. Der Apparat besteht aus vielen komplizierten Einzelteilen. 16. Was ist los? Warum siehst du so traurig aus? 17. Hinter unserem Haus geht eine Bahnlinie vorbei. 18. Hör doch mal hin. Spricht er nicht ausgezeichnet Englisch? 19. Du mußt aber auch immer deine Frau um alles fragen. 20. Irgend jemand läßt aber auch immer das Licht brennen. 21. Ich hoffe, daß du jetzt wirklich offen mit mir redest. 22. Woher stammen Sie? 23. Ich stelle mehr und mehr fest, daß dieses Buch äußerst schwierig ist. 24. Spielen Sie Klavier? 25. Er humpelt, weil er sich gestern den Fuß verstaucht hat. 26. Seine Einstellung geht mir allmählich auf die Nerven.

93 Explain why the past tense is used in the following sentences. Could a) the past progressive form or b) the present perfect simple tense be used in any of the examples?

1. I *didn't* sleep a wink last night.
2. The Mayans *developed* a magnificent architecture.
3. Who *invented* the safety pin?
4. Where *did* you have lunch today?
5. I once *discussed* the problem with Perry.
6. He *used* to sell motorcars.

94 Note the use of the past tense in the following examples, and translate them into German.

1. a) Brown's a killer himself. Suppose he *wasn't*.
   b) Tomorrow is Mrs King's birthday. Suppose we *sent* flowers?
2. a) Anyway it's time you *did* the nails on your right hand.
   b) It's time you *chose* a career.
   c) It is high time that the people born and brought up in the suburbs of Britain *found* a spokesman.
3. a) I don't know. I wish I *did*.
   b) I wish I *had* some children to appreciate me.
   c) I wish you *were* here with us, instead of in the stuffy town.
4. a) I'd rather you *went* now.
   b) I had rather you *paid* me now.
5. a) He acts as if he *knew* English perfectly.
   b) "If only Sadie *was* here," I said tearfully.
   c) If you *knew* what he told me.
   d) If I *knew* he *was* coming tomorrow, I should wait.
6. a) "I think you might offer a reward to anyone who can give information

The Tenses

about the crime," said the detective. "Fifty pounds *was* quite enough, I would think."
b) *Did* you want to look at our higher-priced suits?
c) We *were* wondering whether you *were* going to be at home next Sunday.

Sentences for translation.

| 95 |

1. Angenommen ich täte, was du sagst, was würde dann mit mir passieren? 2. Sie lief, als habe sie Flügel an den Füßen. 3. Ich wünschte, mein Wagen würde nicht immer so klappern. 4. Es wäre mir lieber, du würdest es noch nicht erwähnen. 5. Als wir aus dem Kino kamen, wünschten wir alle, wir hätten den Film nicht gesehen. 6. Es wird allmählich Zeit, daß du das Abendessen fertigmachst. 7. Hätten wir doch bloß getan, was man uns gesagt hat! Dann wäre das nicht passiert. 8. Ich wünschte, ich könnte deinen Optimismus teilen. 9. Angenommen, er sagte dir die Wahrheit. Wie würdest du reagieren? 10. Es ist höchste Zeit, daß wir einen Arzt kommen lassen. 11. Alles schien so unwirklich, als sähe ich mich in einem Dokumentarfilm mitspielen. 12. Ich wünschte, sie wäre jetzt bei mir. 13. Ich kann mich noch genau daran erinnern, als ob es gestern erst gewesen wäre.

Explain the use of the progressive and non-progressive past in the following.

| 96 |

1. a) Bond *dropped* the paper on the floor and *sat* down and slowly *ate* his breakfast and thought about Mr Dupont and Goldfinger.
   b) The man *weaved* his way between the diners to the best table in the room. He *pulled* out two chairs, *snapped* his fingers for the maître d'hôtel and the wine waiter, *spread* two menus in front of them, *exchanged* compliments with Mr Brown and *left* them.
2. People *were killing* other people all the time, all over the world. People *were using* their motorcars to kill with. They *were carrying* infectious diseases around.
3. a) He *was raising* his hand to strike her, when he *stopped* short.
   b) I *was* just *interrupting* him, when a shot *was fired*.
   c) He *was turning* with a chuckle towards the fire, when the door *opened*.
4. a) While the army *was finishing* its manoeuvres on the Salisbury Plains, the Home Fleet *was making* mock war in the Firth of Forth.
   b) Yesterday afternoon he *was reading* the newspaper while his wife *was doing* the housework.
5. a) He *was looking* up into the sky all the time he *was speaking*.
   b) And all the time he *was pressing* the bell.

Observe to what effect the progressive and non-progressive forms can be used in narrative.

| 97 |

1. Mr Dupont *gave* instructions to a steward in a white coat. Two others *were* already *setting* up a card table. Bond *walked* to the rail that surrounded the

The Tenses

roof and *looked* down.
2. Soames *raised* the corner of his lip and *looked* at Bosinny. The architect *was grinning* behind the fumes of his cigarette. Now indeed he *looked* like a buccaneer.
3. The first shot *seemed* to thrust Ben forward, the second to pull him back. Somehow he *was* still *moving*, still on his bicycle, passing the sentry, and the sentry *was* still *shooting* at him.
4. After the meal, which both father and daughter *ate* in nervous silence, de Lipski *lit* a cigar and *blew* the smoke up at the ceiling, watching it hit the wallpaper and disperse in all directions. He *was feeling* well. Despite everything he *was feeling* contented. The meal had been good. "Thank you, my love," he *purred* at Lydia, who *was* methodically *clearing* the table. "That *was* delicious. A stew fit for a king."
5. He *drove* on, cursing, and suddenly it *happened*; suddenly his hands *were trembling* feverishly, his face *was* burning hot, his heart *palpitating* wildly.
6. She *looked* at him, smiling. Then she was in his arms and he *was kissing* her with a fine certainty that surprised him.

98 Sentences for translation.

1. „Finden Sie, daß es kalt ist?" fragte er. Er beugte sich schon über das Feuer und rieb sich die Hände. Er trug eine schäbige braune Strickjacke unter seinem schwarzen Sakko.
2. Er öffnete eine abgegriffene Aktentasche und wühlte darin herum, bis er fand, was er suchte.
3. Er hob die Leiche auf und legte sie an die Mauer in den tieferen Schatten. Er rieb sich die Hände an seinen Kleidern ab, fühlte, ob seine Krawatte geradesaß, und ging weiter zu seinem Hotel.
4. Er sagte, sein Name sei Ashe, aber Leamas wußte, daß er log.
5. Er war gern bereit, den anderen die Schuld zuzuschieben (to blame), aber was tat er denn jetzt? – Er lag da in seinem Bett. Sein Sohn trieb dem Ruin entgegen, sein Land ging vor die Hunde, sein Haus war ein Hospital mit Leuten, die er durch seine Sorglosigkeit verletzt hatte, und er lag untätig in seinem Bett!
6. Es waren so viele Leute da, und es war so laut, und ich war so nervös, daß ich sie zuerst gar nicht sah. Sie saß in einem Nebenzimmer weiter hinten. Ich setzte mich auf einen Hocker an der Theke, von wo ich sie beobachten konnte. Ich wagte es nicht, sehr oft hinzuschauen, und das Licht im Nebenzimmer war nicht sehr gut. Dann stand sie auch schon direkt neben mir. Ich hatte so getan, als läse ich in der Zeitung, und hatte sie deshalb nicht aufstehen sehen.

99 A widely used English school grammar[1] has this to say about the use of the progressive form:

[1] Karl Beilhardt / F. W. Sutton, *Essentials of English Grammar*, Stuttgart 1965.

The Tenses

"The continuous form is used for actions or states which continue only for a limited time
1. if they have started but are not yet finished at the present moment or at a certain time in the past or future
2. a) esp. if two actions are going on at the same time
   b) esp. if one action is going on when another action sets in."

Comment on these "rules" in the light of the following authentic examples.

1. Pickingill *sat* in a rocking chair beside the empty fireplace, and *moved* slowly back and forward as he sipped his tea.
2. The noise the newspaper sellers *made* outside had evidently wakened Mr Sleuth.
3. Prackle still *turned* the pages of his illustrated paper. His voice was normal again.
4. The patrol *talked* as they *walked*, and they *talked* of things that they longed for – of meat and of hot soup and of the richness of butter, of the prettiness of girls and of their smiles and of their lips and their eyes.
5. My foot *itches*. / My foot *is itching*.
6. My arm *aches*. / My arm *is aching*.
7. Mark's shoulder *was throbbing* and his head *ached*.
8. We *were listening* to an interesting play on the radio, while Mother *was preparing* dinner.
9. Bond *searched* the files while he *summed* up the man.
10. The band *played* while I *wrote*.
11. While they *walked* through the woods, the rain *became* worse.
12. And while she *was speaking* thus she *watched* Manning.
13. When they arrived, the hostess *stood* at the door.
14. Who had struck him? Without a doubt Macari who, as I said, *was standing* nearest to him.
15. Julie turned over the leaves of a book that *was lying* on the floor beside her.
16. After a couple of minutes he *walked* back towards the footpath, leaving the parcel where it *lay*.
17. Sir Aubrey *chose* a pipe from the rack that *stood* on his desk and began to fill it.
18. There was nothing to remind them of what had happened, except for a little cloud that still *hung* over the corpse.
19. How charming the yellow curtain looked! His heart *was beating* very fast. He opened the suitcase. His heart *beat* wildly.
20. The sail bellied out and strained ... and the boat flew. – I *steered*. – We had the river to ourselves. We skimmed the water and no one spoke. – I *was steering*.
21. One of them *was holding* a feather brush; the other *carried* four pieces of thick rope.

The Tenses

100 Now go over the examples in **99** once again and try to determine in which cases the simple form could be replaced by the progressive form, and vice versa. In so far as this is possible, can you discover any differences in meaning?

101 Study the following examples carefully, asking yourself why the italicized forms may have been chosen and whether, and with what difference in meaning, they could be replaced by their simple or progressive equivalents.

1. The wound still *hurts* him.
2. He thought: this *isn't hurting* me a bit, it *is* only *making* me feel we *are being* stupid.
3. The commission *failed* to settle the refugee question.
4. He *was failing* to express what he meant.
5. He *was* deliberately *avoiding* her.
6. The bus *was* now *swinging* round Piccadilly Circus and entering Shaftesbury Avenue.
7. He *was* by now *trembling* with wrath.
8. After ten minutes, he *was finding* the edge of the tea chest uncomfortable.
9. What *were* you *doing* at the time of the murder?
10. What *did* he *do* after the murder?
11. Whatever *were* you *doing* in Eastbourne?
12. Somebody *was telling* me about him the other day.
13. I *was driving* from Edinburgh to London yesterday.
14. I *drove* from Folkestone to Dover yesterday.

102 Explain the use of the progressive and simple forms in the following sentences. Are all these sentences "correct", i.e., do the forms used make sense? Point out any sentences that you consider "wrong".

1. a) When I saw him, he *ran* away.
   b) When I saw him, he *was running* away.
2. a) When the police arrived, Richards *barred* the door.
   b) When the police arrived, Richards *was barring* the door.
3. a) They *ate* tacos and salad when the phone rang.
   b) They *were eating* tacos and salad when the phone rang.
4. a) We *swam* while they *played* tennis.
   b) We *were swimming* while they *were playing* tennis.
5. a) My hat *blew off* while I *was crossing* the road.
   b) My hat *was blowing off* while I *was crossing* the road.
6. With cries of joy, the lovers *embraced* while Sir Pellinore *opened* the champagne, and soon Gregory *was telling* Alice of his escape from the camp.
7. Now, come downstairs and have a cup of tea while I *give* you all the details.
8. As the train *pulled* out of the station, Betty *stole* a timid glance at her husband.

The Tenses

9. a) I *painted* the table this morning.
   b) I *was painting* the table this morning.
10. a) My sister *called* on me last night.
    b) My sister *was calling* on me last night.
11. a) I *was talking* to the Prime Minister yesterday.
    b) I *talked* to the Prime Minister yesterday.
12. Well, I *was saying* that country people never walk.
13. Oh dear! I *was writing* him a letter this morning and forgot all about it.
14. I *was reading* a paper tomorrow.
15. Next minute they *were having* their first quarrel.
16. By the time I had finished he *was lighting* his third cigarette.

It is often said in grammar books that to express a habit the simple form is used. Consider, however, the following examples. | 103 |

1. a) When he *was* not *reading*, he *was meeting* her.
   b) If he *was* not *working*, he *was walking*.
2. a) Every morning when he *was having* breakfast, his wife asked him for money.
   b) He only lost his temper **when he *was dining*** out.

Use the past simple or the past progressive form, pointing out cases where either would be correct. | 104 |

1. The cellar (feel) cool. In two minutes I (shiver). In five minutes I (beg) to be taken outside.
2. By this time the schooner and her little consort (glide) swiftly through the water.
3. He (send) it on, but probably hasn't.
4. I (open) the door and (go) in. There was no light in the room. Cohn (lie), face down, on the bed in the dark.
5. I (finish) my training when notice (come) round inviting linguists to apply for special service abroad.
6. He (stand) looking at the body.
7. I asked him if I (interrupt).
8. He said he (lead) a very gay life in London.
9. It did strike me that you (ignore) me rather pointedly at the party.
10. He (wonder) if his brother (have) a bad dream.
11. I occasionally went along on summer evenings and (play) in the backyard or the street while they (talk).
12. Daisy had disappeared, and when her father joined her in the passage she (listen), with downcast eyes, to what Joe Chandler (say). He (tell) her about his real home, of the place where his mother (live), at Richmond – that it was a nice little house, close to the park. He (ask) her whether she could manage

The Tenses

to come out there one afternoon, explaining that his mother would give them both tea, and how nice it would be.
13. While they (wait) for the lift, Bond (glance) out of the tall window at the end of the passage. He (look) down into the deep well of the back courtyard of the bank. A trim chocolate-brown lorry had come into the courtyard through the triple steel gates. Square cardboard boxes (be) unloaded from it, and (be) put on a short conveyor belt that (disappear) into the bowels of the bank.

105 Sentences for translation.

1. Betty, die sich gerade die Haare bürstete, nickte. 2. Langweile ich dich mit meiner Geschichte? 3. Du hattest einen bösen Traum, und ich hielt es für besser, dich zu wecken. 4. Als wir ankamen, aßen sie gerade zu Mittag. 5. Es nieste jemand, während der Präsident sprach. 6. Halte du das Baby, während ich die Flasche wärme!

106 Here is another "rule" from the English grammar quoted in **99**:
"Certain verbs are never used in the continuous form, even in cases where the continuous form would normally be expected:
 a) verbs of perception when used in their normal senses: *to hear, to notice, to see, to smell, to taste*
 b) verbs of liking and disliking: *to dislike, to hate, to like, to love, to mind (I don't mind), to prefer*
 c) verbs expressing a wish: *to desire, to want, to wish*
 d) verbs expressing a belief, an opinion, etc.: *to agree, to believe, to doubt, to feel* (= be of the opinion that), *to know, to remember, to seem, to suppose, to think, to understand*
 e) some verbs expressing a state: *to be, to belong, to contain, to exist, to have* (= possess), *to know, to possess, to own*"

Study the following authentic examples and explain in what way the above rule needs modification.

1. a) Which judge *is hearing* the case?
   b) I'*m* actually *hearing* your voice at last.
   c) I was not sure I *was hearing* right.
2. People *are noticing* you, Ellen.
3. a) The fuse has burnt; George *is seeing* to it.
   b) I'*m* just *seeing* my friend off.
   c) I told myself that I *was seeing* ghosts.
   d) Bob *is seeing* quite a bit of Mary these days.
   e) The audience didn't know whether they *were seeing* a hit or a flop.
4. The place *was smelling* like a dunghill.
5. She *was disliking* the other woman more every minute.

6. a) How I *am hating* his flatteries!
   b) He's *hating* to hear the big no.
7. a) He *was* obviously not *liking* the show at all.
   b) How *are* you *liking* your new job?
8. You should have heard Travis Jablock appealing to my patriotism to get me to change the end of my book. It was heartrending. The two producers and the director in the room with us *were loving* it.
9. I've *been desiring* to speak to this legendary man for years.
10. a) Don't misunderstand me, Major, I'm not bragging. I'm only *wanting* to explain why . . .
    b) I've *been wanting* to speak to you.
11. He was giving her that incredible yarn, and I could see that she *was believing* every word of it.
12. Why am I looking at you? Because I'm *remembering* all the times before when you've tricked me.
13. a) What *are* you *thinking* about? – I'm *thinking* about my dinner.
    b) "Shut up!" Johnny snarled. "I'm *thinking*."
    c) I'm *thinking* it was a mistake after all.
14. a) Except when he *was being* pedantic, he could not be called unpleasant.
    b) I hope you're *being* quite, quite frank with me.
    c) I'm not *being* any woman's pet.

Present perfect and past tense with time indications. – Sentences for observation. **107**

1. a) I *visited* Rome last year.
   b) The rain *stopped* a minute ago.
   c) I scarcely *noticed* her at the party.
2. a) Where *did* you *have* lunch today?
   b) I've *had* a very busy day at the office today.
3. a) I *did* not *look* at the paper this morning.
   b) I *haven't looked* at the paper this morning.
4. a) *Have* you *paid* your rent recently?
   b) He *told* me quite recently that . . .
5. a) I *discussed* the matter lately with a fellow student.
   b) I *have* lately *been* pestered with all kinds of begging letters.
6. a) Until quite recently I always *used* to use Pear's soap.
   b) Until now I've *been* a very busy man.
7. a) *Did* you ever *hear* of such a thing?
   b) *Have* you ever *heard* of such a thing?
8. a) She spoke, as indeed she *has* always *spoken*, simply, clearly and vividly.
   b) She spoke, as indeed she always *spoke*, . . .
9. a) I've already *said* it.
   b) I already *saw* that movie.
10. a) I *have* never *forgotten* our first meeting at the Royal.
    b) I never *spoke* to her in my life.

The Tenses

11. a) I regard him as the greatest benefactor to mankind that *has* ever *lived*.
    b) I regard him as the greatest benefactor to mankind that ever *lived*.
12. a) I repeat what I *said* before.
    b) I repeat what I*'ve said* before.
13. a) He *has lived* with his uncle for some time.
    b) He *lived* with his uncle for some time.
14. a) I *saw* him only once.
    b) I *have seen* him only once.
15. a) After his death she suddenly left London, and she *has* only just *returned*.
    b) Are you tired? — No, no, I only just *got* home.
    c) Who do you think I *saw* just now?
16. a) I *have* scarcely *seen* him during the last (*or:* past) few weeks.
    b) I scarcely *saw* him last week.

108 Present perfect and past tense without time indications. — Sentences for observation.

1. a) *Were* you at Oxford?
   b) *Have* you *been* to Oxford?
2. a) Newton *has explained* the movement of the moon.
   b) Newton *believed* in an omnipotent God.
3. a) England *has had* many able rulers.
   b) Assyria *had* many able rulers.
4. a) America *was discovered* by Columbus.
   b) Though America *has been discovered* by Columbus, Peter von Zahn seems to think that he has to do the whole job over again.
5. a) Hello, Jack, I*'ve come* back to ask you something.
   b) Hello, Jack, I *came* back to ask you something.
6. a) You don't need to shout at me because you don't like the hat I *bought*.
   b) Mary *has bought* a new hat.
7. a) *Did* you *sleep* well?
   b) *Have* you *slept* well?
8. a) How many times *did* you *see* him?
   b) How many times *have* you *seen* him?
9. a) No greater dramatist *came* after him.
   b) No greater dramatist *has come* after him.

109 Point out the differences between the following.

1. a) I *have* sometimes *thought* that I would be better off without a wife.
   b) I sometimes *thought* that I would be better off without a wife.
2. a) One *has been* young.
   b) We *were* all young once.

The Tenses

3. a) Helen *has been* to England.
   b) Helen *is* in England for six months.
   c) Helen *was* in England for six months.
   d) Helen *has been* in England for six months.
4. a) We always *discussed* these things on Thursdays.
   b) We *have* always *discussed* these things on Thursdays.
5. a) He *lived* in this village all his life.
   b) He *has lived* in this village all his life.
6. a) My father *has lived* through three wars.
   b) My father *lived* through three wars.
7. a) Fortune *has* always *smiled* on him.
   b) Fortune always *smiled* on him.
8. a) He's never *seen* the Niagara Falls.
   b) He never *saw* the Niagara Falls.
9. a) He *has made* many memorable speeches.
   b) He *made* many memorable speeches.

Add the adverbials given in brackets and make any necessary changes in tense. | 110 |

1. I've cut my finger. (this morning) 2. They've broken the window. (when they were playing ball) 3. They've caught the robber. (in a deserted old farmhouse) 4. We've sold our house. (last spring) 5. Jack's been in town for a week. (last autumn) 6. Have you seen Inspector Smith? (at the meeting) 7. I have written to him several times. (when I was in England) 8. Where the hell have you been? (when I called) 9. Has he talked to him? (yesterday) 10. He has written several new poems. (during his stay in Italy)

Are all of the following sentences grammatically and idiomatically correct? | 111 |

1. When I *have asked* a London policeman the way, I *have* invariably *received* a polite answer.
2. Men's hairs *have grown* grey in a single night.
3. My grandmother *has sung* that song.
4. I've *heard* my grandmother sing that song.
5. Specimens of iron *have been* found in Egypt as far back as 2500 B.C.
6. I've *given* up that idea long ago.
7. They're the sort of circle I've always *had*, at the University. – But you left the University long ago.
8. Many a good ship *has gone* down in the past.
9. The rain *stopped* about two minutes ago. – So it *has*.
10. Yesterday, however, Labour's principal spokesmen were unwilling to anticipate the agonizing issue they will have to face. Mr Harold Wilson shied away from the subject on his return from New York. Asked about the succession, he said: "I don't think we can begin to think about that when the leader *has died* only a few hours ago."

The Tenses

112 Present perfect. – Sentences for observation.

1. He *has* long *been* dead.
2. *Has* he *been* here long?
3. How long *have* you *been* in Germany?
4. *Have* you *known* him long?
5. Mary's *had* a headache all morning.

113 Sentences for translation.

1. Ist er schon lange tot? 2. Wie lange sind Sie schon in London? 3. Ich kenne Herrn Jones schon sehr lange. 4. Wie lange bist du schon zurück? 5. Ich kann kaum glauben, daß ich erst einen Tag in England bin. 6. Dieses Denkmal steht schon 50 Jahre hier. 7. Hier ist die Leiche des Mannes, Herr Kommissar. Er muß schon ein paar Stunden tot sein. 8. (Im Konzert:) Es ist das erste Mal, daß ich dieses Musikstück höre.

114 Simple versus progressive form – what is the difference?

1. a) He *has painted* the house.
   b) He *has been painting* the house.
2. a) I've *cleaned* the car.
   b) I've *been cleaning* the car.
3. a) What *have* you *done*?
   b) What *have* you *been doing*?
4. a) Well, we *have* perhaps *spoilt* her a little.
   b) Well, we *have* perhaps *been spoiling* her a little.
5. a) I *have persuaded* my aunt to let me wear those jewels.
   b) I *have* for some time *been persuading* my aunt to wear those jewels.
6. a) Where *have* you *met* her?
   b) Where *have* you *been meeting* her?
7. a) He *has visited* London.
   b) He *has been visiting* London.
8. a) She *has slept* for eight hours.
   b) She *has been sleeping* for eight hours.

115 Account for the use and non-use of the progressive form in cases such as the following.

1. a) We've *had* this car for six months now.
   b) We've *been having* fine weather for the past few days.
2. a) *Have* you *known* them for a long time?
   b) *Have* you *been watching* them for a long time?

The Tenses

116 Try to explain why the present perfect progressive tense is used in the following examples. What other tenses, if any, could have been used instead, and would such changes in tense have affected the meaning?

1. I've just *been getting* some last-minute presents I forgot.
2. I've *been thinking*. – About what?
3. You've *been travelling* about, I understand. – Yes, I've been in Haiti, and Mexico.
4. You've *been having* rather more trouble than I thought, haven't you?
5. Redlitch: Do you know me?
   Gillian: I've seen your picture on your book. Come in, won't you? This is Mr Henderson. Mr Shepherd Henderson.
   Redlitch: Oh – you've *been writing* to me.
   Shepherd: And you've *not been answering*. How do you do?
6. Martin, you're in one of your silly moods. *Have* you *been drinking* again?
7. You've *been working* too hard.
8. Your son's *been having* trouble with his arithmetic.

117 Study the following sentences carefully. Are any of them grammatically or idiomatically objectionable?

1. Since his own book was published, he's *been noticing* misprints in others much more.
2. For a number of years I've *been seeing* myself as a sort of rolling stone, a fascinating freelance, a man of infinite possibilities.
3. The parents looked to me suspiciously like character actors I *have been seeing* in Soviet films since 1929.
4. I've *been wanting* to get in touch with you for a good many months.
5. I've *been wishing* to do this for a long time.

118 Present perfect simple or present perfect progressive? Where either form seems possible, point out whether or not there is a difference in meaning.

1. He has (work) hard lately. 2. Our goods (sell) well lately. 3. I (read) since three. 4. Someone (move) my books. 5. Mr Soames lands at Southampton tonight. – He always (come), but so far he has always been prevented. 6. We (have) a few thefts lately. 7. The days (get) warmer of late. 8. I (come) here for four months. 9. I (mean) to buy myself a new pipe. 10. I just (read) your poems. 11. I (think) about it. 12. Christ, Sid, you (read) too many books. 13. All night long I (dream) about this breakfast. 14. You (see) too many of these degenerate American movies in Austria. 15. I (ache) to kiss you for the last three hours. 16. You may think I (change), but I'm still the same man I always

The Tenses

was. 17. Why the light (go) out? 18. There was the smell of cigarette smoke in the air. "Who (smoke)?" she asked. 19. What you (do) all these months? 20. You (watch) too much TV. 21. I not (laugh) so much for years. 22. I (know) him all my life. 23. He (want) to go home to bed for more than an hour. 24. He (travel) lately.

119 Judging from the following examples, what difference, if any, is there between the simple form and the progressive form of *live*?

1. We *live* in London.
2. We're *living* in London at the moment.
3. The Johnsons *live* in New Jersey now.
4. While I *was living* in Africa, I went on a lion hunt.
5. How long *have* you *been living* here in White Plains?
6. How long *has* Bill *lived* in New York?
7. He *has been living* in India for twenty years.
8. He *has lived* in India for twenty years.
9. I've *been living* here now for four years – ever since my father died.

120 Structures with *since*. – Study the following authentic examples, all of which are perfectly natural and idiomatic English. Say which of them deviate from the "rules" established so far, and try to find explanations for these seemingly unorthodox usages.

1. a) Since he *has got* on in the world, he *has grown* snobbish.
   b) Since I *have been* at this school, we *have had* three headmasters.
   c) He *has* never *been* to visit me since *I've been* ill.
2. a) What else *have* men *done*, since the world *began*?
   b) Since I last *wrote* to you, a lot *has happened*.
   c) I *have* never *seen* my boy since he *was* a baby.
3. a) He *is going* to work by bus since his car *broke down*.
   b) I'm *hearing* much better since I *had* that operation.
4. We're *eating* more meat since the war.
5. a) Since the First World War this *is* no longer true.
   b) Since his accident he *walks* with a limp.
6. a) Things *have been* very difficult in this country since the war, especially for people with small incomes.
   b) A lot of water *has flowed* under the bridge since then.
7. a) It's a long time since I *saw* you.
   b) It's a long time since you and I *had* a good gossip.
   c) It *is* less than half a century since the Wright brothers *were experimenting* with their machine, and today the chief cities of the world are linked by a network of air routes.

8. a) It's nearly three years since I've had a new dress.
   b) It's nine hours since I've eaten anything.
   c) It's a long time since we've been to the country.
9. a) Since when *is* an artist supposed to be St Francis of Assisi?
   b) Since when *does* a rabbit have claws?
   c) Since when *does* a general have to appeal to his officers to attack?
   d) Since when *do* you know Redlitch?
10. a) Since when *has* he *been* missing?
    b) Since when *have* you *had* second sight?
    c) Since when *have* we *had* passports?
11. a) He *wrote* like nobody else at the time, and nobody *has written* like him since.
    b) I've *had* a guilty conscience about it ever since.

Sentences for translation. **121**

1. Seit er verheiratet ist, ist er vernünftiger geworden. 2. Ich bin schon seit Tagesanbruch auf den Beinen. 3. Es ist lange her, seit ich dich zum letztenmal gesehen habe. 4. Ich bin schon seit vorgestern hier. 5. Ich habe ihn seitdem nicht mehr gesehen. 6. Diese Wohnung macht mich noch verrückt. Seitdem du fortgegangen bist, ist hier einfach die Hölle los: der Mann von oben spielt dauernd Posaune, und sein widerlicher kleiner Junge übt dazu Klavier. 7. Seit wann muß ich dich fragen, ob ich rauchen darf? 8. Wie lange ist es her, seit Sie in London waren? 9. Es ist lange her, seit wir uns unterhalten haben. 10. Wie lange ist es her, daß Sie eine Gehaltserhöhung bekommen haben? 11. Himmel nochmal! Seit wann sind Sie so kleinlich? 12. Er ist immer sehr geschwätzig gewesen, solange ich ihn kenne. 13. Seit meiner Krankheit trinke ich kaum noch Bier. 14. Es ist schon lange her, seit du bei uns warst.

Miscellaneous sentences for translation. **122**

1. Ich habe ihm schon mehrmals geschrieben. 2. Ich habe ihm eben geschrieben. 3. Wo bist du die letzten acht Tage gewesen? 4. Wo bist du vorige Woche gewesen? 5. (Beim Aufwachen:) Wie lange habe ich geschlafen? 6. Es ist das erste Mal, daß Bill versucht hat, jemanden zu heiraten. 7. Er arbeitet nun schon seit heute morgen um acht. 8. Ich suche dich nun schon seit einer halben Stunde. 9. Sie hintergeht ihn nun schon seit Monaten. 10. Wie lange kennst du Henry eigentlich schon? 11. Wie lange trägt er schon eine Brille? 12. Wie lange ist Frankreich schon eine Republik? 13. Diese Vögel kommen nun schon seit langem jedes Jahr hierher zurück. 14. Herr Hill unterrichtet nun schon seit fünf Jahren am hiesigen Gymnasium. 15. Ich habe den Schlüssel wiedergefunden, den ich gestern verloren hatte. 16. Haben Sie die Pyramiden gesehen, als Sie in Ägypten waren, oder haben Sie sich nur für die politische Lage interessiert? 17. Brown hat seinem Nachbarn längst vergeben, aber er hat ihn lange gehaßt und verabscheut. 18. Bis heute war ich leider zu beschäftigt, um von Ihrer Ein-

The Tenses

ladung Gebrauch zu machen. 19. Seit eh und je ist Kölns Eigenart der Ausdruck seines Standortes. 20. Es ist das erste Mal, daß ich mich in den Händen der Polizei befinde. 21. Wann sind Sie in die Partei eingetreten? 22. Deshalb habe ich die ganze Zeit nichts von ihm gehört. 23. England ist nicht mehr das, was es war. 24. Es gab eine Zeit, da warst du froh, wenn du trockenes Brot zu essen hattest. 25. Damals fuhr ich noch mit dem Bus zur Arbeit. 26. Er humpelt, weil er sich heute morgen beim Fußballspielen den Knöchel verstaucht hat. 27. Wie ich höre, mein Sohn, hast du in letzter Zeit wieder allerlei angestellt. 28. Ich habe den ganzen Tag im Garten gearbeitet. 29. Während die Frauen das Essen zubereiteten, unterhielten wir Männer uns im Wohnzimmer über Politik. 30. Die beste Freundin meiner Tochter ist auf ein paar Tage zu uns gekommen. Als sie gestern abend ankam, verlor sie völlig die Fassung, denn es ist das erste Mal, daß sie hier ist, seit ihr Mann gestorben ist.

123 Past perfect. – Compare and distinguish.

1. a) Towards noon we *reached* the top of the mountain.
   b) Towards noon we *had reached* the top of the mountain.
2. a) When we came out of the theatre, the rain *stopped*.
   b) When we came out of the theatre, the rain *had stopped*.
3. a) When the police arrived, the man *was* dead.
   b) When the police arrived, the man *had been* dead for at least two hours.
4. a) When she entered the room, her husband *poured* himself another whisky.
   b) When she entered the room, her husband *had drunk* most of the whisky.
   c) When she entered the room, she found that her husband *had* evidently *been drinking*.
   d) When she entered the room, she found that her husband *had* evidently *been drinking* for some time.
5. a) After the two of you *had parted*, where did you go?
   b) I didn't see him again after *he went* to prison.
6. a) When he *got* the letter, he burnt it without looking at it.
   b) When he *had read* the letter, he burnt it.

124 Sentences for translation.

1. Als mein Mann nach Hause kam, war ich schon zwei Stunden im Bett. 2. Als ich ihn das letzte Mal traf, war er noch nicht lange verheiratet. 3. Wie lange waren Sie schon in England, als Sie die Nachricht von seinem Tode erhielten? 4. Seit sie Arthur kannte, hatte er nie mit ihr über seine Kindheit gesprochen. 5. Ich war schon lange in sie verliebt, aber ich hatte es noch nie gewagt, sie einzuladen, mit mir auszugehen. 6. Etwa drei Wochen, nachdem Leamas seine Arbeit in der Bibliothek aufgenommen hatte, lud ihn Elizabeth zum Abendessen ein. 7. Erinnern Sie sich nicht, daß Sie jemand ansprach, nachdem Sie Ihr Büro verlassen hatten? 8. Es war das erste Mal, daß ich ihn so ratlos sah.

The Tenses

125 Ways of expressing futurity. – Are all of the following sentences equally idiomatic? Try to differentiate between them.

1. When *will* you *do* your shopping?
2. When *are* you *going to do* your shopping?
3. When *are* you *doing* your shopping?
4. When *will* you *be doing* your shopping?
5. When *will* you *be going to do* your shopping?
6. When *do* you *do* your shopping?

126 Would you regard any of the following sentences as unidiomatic or downright "wrong"? Give reasons. (For the uses of *will* cf. **172**; for the uses of *shall* cf. **175**.)

1. Sometimes I think I *will be* glad when it is over.
2. When you get this letter, I *will be* a dead man.
3. *Will* I *see* you tomorrow?
4. *Will* I *get* better?
5. What *will* we *have* for dinner?
6. Are you coming voluntarily, or *will* I *have* to force you?
7. I *will do* it if you *will help* me.
8. I shall be grateful if you *will return* it soon.
9. If you*'ll be* kind enough to wait a moment more, I *will see* if an appointment can be arranged for you.
10. I only hope nobody *comes*.
11. I hope you *get* well soon.
12. I hope you *get* the job.
13. I doubt if we *meet* again.

127 What difference, if any, would it make if *shall* were replaced by *will* in the following passage?

We *shall* not *flag* or *fail*. We *shall fight* in France, we *shall fight* on the seas and oceans, we *shall fight* with growing confidence and growing strength in the air, we *shall defend* our island, whatever the cost may be, we *shall fight* on the beaches, we *shall fight* on the landing grounds, we *shall fight* in the fields and in the streets, we *shall fight* in the hills; we *shall* never *surrender*. (Winston Churchill)

128 What does *will* express in each of the following sentences?

1. That*'ll be* the postman.
2. That *will be* twenty dollars, please.
3. You *will address* me as Dr Koenig at all times and otherwise show the respect due to a superior.

The Tenses

4. Students intending to take this examination *will sign* the list in the office of the secretary.

129 Sentences for observation.
1. a) She *starts* for Chicago tomorrow evening.
   b) We *leave* for Liverpool a week today.
   c) "We *go* home tomorrow," Jeremy announced.
   d) When *do* we go to London?
   e) The lease *expires* in 1975.
   f) Who *do* we tackle first?
   g) What time *do* the reporters get there?
   h) Tomorrow I *start* writing a new book.
2. a) He *is playing* in the concert tonight.
   b) I'm *leaving* on the 7 o'clock plane tonight.
   c) He's *addressing* the conference on Tuesday.
   d) I'm *going* shopping in a minute.
   e) He's *retiring* at the end of the term.
   f) I'm *seeing* that film next week.
   g) When *are* you *meeting* him? – Soon.
   h) It's stopped raining. I'm *going* for a walk. *Are* you *coming* with me?
3. a) I'm *going to* see a game of football this afternoon.
   b) I'm *going to* be sick.
   c) I'm fed up with being talked about. I'm *not going to* be talked about any more by anyone.
   d) Not a drop of blood *is going to* be shed, or you'll be held responsible.
   e) He says he's *going to* win, and he isn't such a bad prophet, is he?
   f) Lovely weather we're having. It's *going to* be hot again today.
   g) This *is going to* cost you a lot of money.
   h) I'm *going to* find out if you can swim or not.

130 Compare and distinguish.
1. He: "There isn't any ink in the house."
   She: a) "I'm *going to get* some today."
        b) "I'll *get* some today."
2. a) I'm *seeing* my girl friend tomorrow.
   b) I'll *be seeing* my girl friend tomorrow.
3. a) I'm *meeting* him tomorrow.
   b) I'll *be meeting* him tomorrow (next year, some time).
   c) I'll *be meeting* him.
4. a) *Will* you *be going* to the post office?
   b) *Will* you *go* to the post office?
5. a) You *will work* in this department under Mr Jones.
   b) You *will be working* in this department under Mr Jones.

The Tenses

Choose what you consider the most likely forms. | **131**

1. Tomorrow (I, I'll) apply for a job with the Times. 2. (I, I'll) call and see you when (I, I'll) come to London. 3. Call again this afternoon, when (I have, I'll have) more time to see you. 4. Go to the main entrance, where (you, you'll) find a messenger waiting. 5. And when (do, will) I hear from you? 6. (I, I'll) get on the first bus that (comes, will come) along. 7. You're to bring me the papers which (you, you'll) find on my desk. 8. I'm sure you (don't, won't) object if (I, I'll) move the ashtray. 9. I fear the house (does, will) not survive the storms of another winter. 10. I hope (we, we'll) stay here for fifty years!

Fill in *will*, *shall*, or *be going to*, adjusting the word order where necessary. | **132**

1. I think it ..... rain today. 2. Don't you know that I ..... never leave you? 3. ..... you take that job? 4. I'm crazy about you, Gillian, when ..... we get married? 5. I swear that I ..... not practise witchcraft ever in this house again. 6. ..... we ever hear from them again? 7. You think you ..... like America? 8. I ..... never set foot in Germany again. 9. When ..... you get some comfortable furniture into this room? 10. ..... we ever be able to come back here? 11. We ..... have to make up our minds what sort of house we want. 12. ..... I be able to find the place?

Interpret the following uses of *be going to*. | **133**

1. What *were* you *going to say*?
2. You *were going to tell* us what happened.
3. My father *was going to take* me to Ireland once. But then he went away by himself.
4. I *was going to give* it to you last night, but I didn't see you.
5. My wife *was going to have* a new dress made, but she has changed her mind.

Study the following passage, in which *will* and *'ll* is used throughout to express futurity. Do you think that *be going to* could be used instead? | **134**

Dave *will marry* some girl who's in love with him. Oh, he*'ll fight* every inch of the way, of course. Then there*'ll be* children and he*'ll be* free to do as he likes. He*'ll have* a succession of girls, and in between each one he*'ll go* back and weep on his wife's shoulder because of his unfortunately weak character. She*'ll forgive* him all right. He*'ll* even *use* her compliance as an additional attraction for the little girls. My wife understands me, he*'ll say*, with a sloppy look at his wife. She*'ll* always *be* there to take me back.

Compare and distinguish. | **135**

1. a) When *will* we *get* married?
   b) When *shall* we *get* married?

The Tenses

2. a) *Will* you *go* to the seaside with us?
   b) *Will* you *be going* to the seaside with us?
3. a) He will let us know when the plane *arrives*.
   b) He will let us know when the plane *will arrive*.
4. a) If I have to wait much longer, I *will* never *see* the New World.
   b) Come what may, *I'm going to see* the New World.
5. a) The doctors had little doubt that he *was going to die*.
   b) You, too, *will die* some day.
6. a) You*'ll regret* this.
   b) *You're going to regret* this.
7. a) In a few years *I'm opening* a branch out in the country.
   b) In a few years *I'm going to open* a branch out in the country.
8. a) *I'm reading* a paper tomorrow.
   b) I *was reading* a paper tomorrow.
9. a) He *is taking* the examination in June.
   b) He *was taking* the examination in June.
10. a) *Will* you *come*?
    b) *Are* you *coming*?
11. a) He*'s coming* to see us next week.
    b) He*'s* always *coming* to see us next week.
12. a) *Will* you *come* tomorrow?
    b) *Will* you *be coming* tomorrow?
13. a) *Are* you *going to have* your breakfast in bed?
    b) *Will* you *be having* your breakfast in bed?
14. a) *Will* you *lecture* in English?
    b) *Are* you *going to lecture* in English?
    c) *Will* you *be lecturing* in English?
15. a) She *won't make* the beds.
    b) She *won't be making* the beds.
    c) She *isn't going to make* the beds.

136 To what extent, and with what differences in meaning, could other forms be used to express futurity in the following sentences?

1. She *won't be coming* in tomorrow night, so we*'ll have* a party all on our own.
2. You*'ll be hearing* from me.
3. I *shall be seeing* him when I go up to London in a day or two.
4. The fall semester *will be starting* soon.
5. It's nothing to worry about, but *I'll be needing* more money.

137 Interpret the following sentences.

1. We*'ll knock off* now.   You*'ll be wanting* your teas like me.
2. I*'ll be* down at the post at eight.

3. And now you'*ll be wanting* to wash up.
4. You'*ll be wanting* more definite information than that, won't you?
5. I expect the Captain *will be wanting* to get on the move.
6. You'*ll be wondering* why I'm late.

What does the *will (shall) be* + *-ing* form express in the following examples? **138**

1. Tell me what you'*ll be doing* on Christmas Day.
2. When I get back, they'*ll be having* dinner.
3. When I reach London, it *will* probably *be raining*.
4. In a few minutes I *shall be seeing* him, *talking* to him, *telling* him that I love him.
5. I imagine they'*ll be saying* their prayers any moment now.
6. Soon you *will be saying* that I am a Red.
7. On your way now, or you'*ll be saying* I kept you late.

Insert the appropriate forms, making any necessary adjustments in word order. **139**

1. I'm determined he (not come) here again. 2. I imagine you (celebrate) tonight. 3. You (report) to the principal at once. 4. You (fetch) me a glass of water? 5. We do not know when he (come), but when he (come), he will not find us ungrateful. 6. I expect you (spend) some time in Paris next week. 7. You (wonder) why I am so late. 8. I hope he (win) by a fantastic margin. 9. I (get) in touch with the newspaper tomorrow. But under the circumstances I can't. 10. I'm afraid I can't talk it over with you now, because I have to take these parcels to the post office. – I (come) with you. 11. Excuse me, sir, the bar (close) in a few minutes. 12. I (start) work tomorrow. 13. I (see) you soon? 14. You (be) the first to be told. 15. The new road bridge (be) opened this summer, when the Queen (make) a speech. 16. It (not be) a private conversation. 17. You children (stay) here until I come back. 18. According to the timetable we (leave) on Tuesday and we (return) two days later. 19. You (leave) without paying? 20. I (leave) the flowers at the hospital for you. I (go) there anyway to visit my mother. 21. Perhaps the letter (arrive) today. 22. What beautiful weather we're having. It (be) hot again today. 23. The Prime Minister (talk) on TV tonight. 24. That (cost) a pretty penny. 25. She always (write) in a few days, but I never get any mail from her. 26. I see you've bought Joyce's *Ulysses*. You really (read) it? 27. When you (do) your shopping? 28. The exams (start) next week. 29. You (help) me write these letters? 30. In August I (holiday) in the Scillies as usual.

Sentences for translation. **140**

1. Das schreibe ich mir auf. 2. Ich erzähle Ihnen jetzt eine Geschichte, die ich selbst erlebt habe. 3. Ich fahre morgen nach Paris. 4. Wir ziehen bald aufs Land. 5. Kommst du morgen? 6. In die nächste Woche fällt der Geburtstag eines der

The Tenses

größten Erfinder. 7. Du wirst mich doch wohl nicht in der Tinte sitzen lassen? 8. Ich glaube nicht, daß er bis zum Kaffee wieder hier ist. 9. Kommt der Kerl eigentlich überhaupt nicht? 10. Beeile dich, oder du kommst zu spät. 11. Das wird wohl der Herr sein, der in der vorigen Woche schon einmal vorgesprochen hat. 12. Sobald er zurückkommt, sage ich ihm Bescheid. 13. Ich werde dir regelmäßig schreiben. 14. Ich bleibe nicht lange weg. 15. Vielleicht kommt der Brief heute an. 16. Morgen kommen die Klempner, um das Waschbecken im Badezimmer in Ordnung zu bringen. 17. Leider bin ich nicht lange hier. 18. Bis Montag habe ich das Buch aus. 19. Ich werde den ganzen Sommer über auf einem Bauernhof arbeiten. 20. Wann beginnen die Sommerferien? 21. Was machst du morgen? 22. Ich komme Sie um acht Uhr abholen. – Nein, dann bin ich wahrscheinlich noch beim Frühstück. 23. Mein Vater wird im März fünfundsechzig. 24. Es ist sicher, daß er sein Examen besteht. 25. Werden Sie lange in London bleiben? 26. Wann heiratet ihr? 27. Er wird Lehrer. 28. Sie bekommt ein Kind. 29. In ein bis zwei Stunden ist alles vorbei. 30. Wann sehe ich dich wieder? 31. Sage ihm, daß ich ihn um vier Uhr erwarte. 32. Wie lange werden Sie bleiben? 33. Wie lange willst du bleiben? 34. Morgen früh werden wir wissen, ob er wiedergewählt ist. 35. Er tritt nächstes Jahr in den Ruhestand. 36. Was wirst du morgen um diese Zeit machen? 37. Am 21. Oktober sind wir 25 Jahre verheiratet. 38. Um diese Zeit nächstes Jahr habe ich 50 Pfund gespart. 39. Wir werden dich hier vermissen. 40. Er läßt sich den Zahn am Freitag ziehen. 41. Werde ich jemals wieder gehen können? 42. Er wird geschimpft haben.

141 Correct the following sentences where necessary.

1. If you go with him, he is going to give you a new one tomorrow. 2. If you'll wait here for a moment, I'll fetch a chair. 3. She is buying a new hat next autumn. 4. Stay here until he will come back. 5. Wait till Tuesday, when I shall tell you everything. 6. I can't fix the time yet when I'm able to leave. 7. I shall try to persuade him to do it before it will be too late. 8. I hope you get well soon. 9. I doubt if we ever meet again. 10. She was going to go on working at the studio for another month or two. 11. I must be going now. My wife will already wait for me. 12. When will I see you again?

142 Conditional sentences. – Point out the differences between the following.

1. If she *wants* to go on working, she *will / can / may / might / could / must / should / ought to* get a job locally.
2. If she *wanted* to go on working, she *would / could / might / should / ought to* get a job locally.
3. If she *had wanted* to go on working, she *would / could / might / should / ought to* have got a job locally.

The Tenses

Compare. **143**

1. a) I'*ll go* with him if he *asks* me to.
   b) I'*ll go* with him if he *should ask* me to.
2. a) If he *should* call, tell him to wait.
   b) *Should* he call, tell him to wait.
3. a) If I *saw* him, I'*d speak* to him.
   b) If I *were to* see him, I'*d speak* to him.
4. a) If I *had known* you were busy, I *wouldn't have bothered* you.
   b) *Had* I *known* you were busy, I *wouldn't have bothered* you.
5. a) If there *were* a chance you might listen, I'*d try* to make you understand.
   b) If there *was* a chance you might listen, I'*d try* to make you understand.
6. a) If you *wrote* to him on my behalf, I'*d be* greatly obliged to you.
   b) If you *would write* to him on my behalf, I'*d be* greatly obliged to you.
7. a) If you *had gone* to England, you *would have learnt* the language properly.
   b) If you *had gone* to England, you *would* now *speak* the language properly.
8. a) You'*ll have* to pay more if you *buy* it on hire-purchase.
   b) You always *pay* more if you *buy* something on hire-purchase.

Comment on the following sentences. **144**

1. I *wouldn't like* to be in your shoes if my father *comes* round.
2. If my allowing you to hypnotize me *is going to lead* to your dominating my mind, I'*d prefer* to put up with the pain.
3. If ever I *become* rich, I'*d move* to London and *spend* my declining days cultivating good companions and good food.
4. If we *got* to them at once, they *may commission* you to write the articles.
5. If they *wouldn't give* it to him, he *ran* the risk of being locked up and put back across the border.
6. If you *will make* a fool of yourself, I *can't stop* you.
7. If he *left* London yesterday, he *will be* in time for the conference.

Put in the appropriate forms, adjusting the word order where necessary. **145**

1. I wouldn't worry if I (be) you. 2. If you (speak) to her like a father should, I shouldn't have to try and knock some sense into her head. 3. If the earth were flat, any star above it (be) visible from any point on it. 4. I wouldn't do it if I (not like) it. 5. If you (eat) breakfast in England, you would be having eggs and bacon. 6. I don't know what your mother would say if you (go) without your present. 7. If Joyce (watch), he would have cleaned his teeth first. 8. If she can't catch a train, she (take) a taxi. 9. If I'd wanted to go, I (go). 10. If our present society were a sincerely Christian one, there (be) a general conviction that death has been vanquished. 11. If you (like) to talk in the back room, you won't be disturbed. 12. If he does take the job in Australia, I (not see) him

The Tenses

again. 13. I have – if you (pardon) the expression – the distinct feeling you're trying to tell me something. 14. If I stopped talking, there (be) an ugly black silence. 15. If George had been listening, he (understand). 16. There's never time, is there? If it isn't one thing, it (be) another. 17. Of course, you could have a beer if you (want) it. 18. At school, every report card he got carried the legend, "He could do much better if he only (try)." 19. If you only (take) the normal lunch break, you would not have time to go shopping. 20. I think it's better if you (not come) and see us again.

146 Sentences for translation.

1. Wenn ich zum Arzt gehen will, dann suche ich mir selber einen. 2. Wenn es morgen schön wird, dann gehen wir spazieren. 3. Sie könnte uns helfen, wenn sie nur wollte. 4. Wenn ihr hier schon zwanzig Jahre lebt, habt ihr sicher einen großen Freundeskreis. 5. Wenn es dir nicht gefällt, kannst du es jederzeit umtauschen. 6. Wenn die Stadt einen Flugplatz hätte, wäre alles leichter. 7. Wenn seine Frau auch arbeitete, hätten sie mehr Geld zum Ausgeben. 8. Wenn ich Engländer wäre, brauchte ich kein Englisch zu lernen. 9. Ich täte das nicht, wenn ich du wäre. 10. Wenn er hier wäre, wäre es sicher nicht so langweilig. 11. Wenn ich hier jetzt nicht unterrichtete, dann würde ich jetzt auf irgendeiner tropischen Insel in der Sonne liegen. 12. Wenn Shakespeare heute lebte, würde er wahrscheinlich Stücke fürs Fernsehen schreiben. 13. Wenn er käme, müßtest du mich rufen. 14. Wenn ich mehr Englisch könnte, dann könnte ich hier vielleicht arbeiten. 15. Sollte er es doch tun wollen, so müßtest du versuchen, ihn davon abzubringen. 16. Wenn ich mehr Geld hätte, dann hätte ich keinen Morris Minor gekauft. 17. Wenn er intelligenter wäre, wäre er für den Posten in Frage gekommen. 18. Er könnte immer noch am Leben sein, wenn er früher zum Arzt gegangen wäre. 19. Wäre Beethoven Schlagerkomponist gewesen, dann wäre er als reicher Mann gestorben. 20. Wenn du das Paket richtig adressiert hättest, hätte es nicht so lange gebraucht. 21. Wenn du rechtzeitig gekommen wärest, wäre es nicht so schwierig gewesen, dir ein Zimmer zu besorgen. 22. Er wäre nicht so früh gestorben, wenn er öfter zum Arzt gegangen wäre. 23. Er hätte die Stellung nie bekommen, wenn er sich nicht so bemüht hätte. 24. Wenn ich mehr Geld gehabt hätte, dann hätte ich nicht in der letzten Reihe gesessen. 25. Wenn ich geschnarcht hätte, dann wäre er jetzt nicht so guter Laune. 26. Wenn er gerade gearbeitet hätte, dann hätte ich ihn nicht gestört. 27. Hätte ich den wahren Sachverhalt gekannt, so hätte ich anders gehandelt. 28. Ich hätte es schaffen können, wenn ich Spikes-Reifen (studded tyres) gehabt hätte. 29. Er hätte des Verbrechens nicht überführt werden können, wenn sein Hauptkomplize nicht geschnappt worden wäre. 30. Den Fehler hättest du nicht zu machen brauchen, wenn du ein bißchen mehr nachgedacht hättest. 31. Er hätte es sicher richtig gemacht, wenn er es sich hätte erklären lassen. 32. Wären die Juwelen nicht versichert gewesen, dann hätte man sich mehr bemüht, sie wieder herbeizuschaf-

fen. 33. Ich hätte meiner Frau ja beim Abwaschen geholfen, wenn die Sportnachrichten nicht gewesen wären. 34. Wenn Napoleon nicht gewesen wäre, hätte die europäische Geschichte einen anderen Verlauf genommen. 35. Ich wäre Ihnen dankbar, wenn Sie mir Ihren Kostenvoranschlag so bald wie möglich schicken würden. 36. Ich hänge die Bilder auf, wenn du so nett sein willst, die Leiter zu halten. 37. Wenn Sie mir einen Gefallen tun würden, wäre ich Ihnen sehr verbunden. 38. Wenn du dich nicht mehr anstrengst, wird man dich 'rausschmeißen. 39. Ich kann dir das Geld geben, vorausgesetzt, daß du es mir bis zum Ersten zurückgibst. 40. Angenommen, ich hätte dich um das Geld gebeten, hättest du es mir gegeben?

How could the following sentences best be translated into German? | **147**

1. If you're *going to attack* the memory of a distinguished old man, you'll want something more solid than implications.
2. If a metropolitan newspaper *is going to stay* on the streets, it has to have mass circulation.
3. If I'm *going to be* a good reporter, I've got to take threats as a matter of course.

Reported speech. – Sentences for observation. | **148**

1. a) "I know what she means."
   b) He said (that) he knew what she meant.
2. a) "Why doesn't she apply for the job?"
   b) He wanted to know why she didn't apply for the job.
3. a) "Is she staying at the Falcon Hotel?"
   b) He asked if (whether) she was staying at the Falcon Hotel.
4. a) "All men are mortal."
   b) He reminded us that all men are mortal.
5. a) "The food tasted terrible."
   b) He complained that the food had tasted terrible.
6. a) "I have known it all along."
   b) He boasted that he had known it all along.
7. a) "Our experts will find a solution to the problem."
   b) He promised that their experts would find a solution to the problem.
8. a) "Where shall I put it?"
   b) He wanted to know where he was (supposed) to put it.
9. a) "Don't go out at night."
   b) They were warned not to go out at night.
10. a) "Please don't drive too fast."
    b) She urged him not to drive too fast.

The Tenses

149 Reported speech. – Compare the two versions of "A Classroom Discussion".

Mr Smith: The topic that has been suggested for today's discussion is: "Were past generations happier than we are today?"
Natalie: How can we be expected to discuss such a question? After all, we didn't live in the past, did we? How are we to know what life was like in the past?

Paul: I don't agree with Natalie. All of us, at one time or other, have asked ourselves what life might have been like in the past, and we have wondered whether our ancestors were happier than we are today or not.

Ruth: Well roared, lion!
Paul: Don't be sarcastic!
Ruth: I was not being sarcastic. That was my way of expressing agreement. We know a great deal about life in the past and I think we really ought to discuss the question and do away with the myth of the "good old days".

Paul: A rotten time they must have had, without running water, electricity, motorcars, and the National Health Service.

George: Not forgetting radio, motion pictures, and television.

Natalie: I'm not so sure that motorcars, television, motion pictures, and all the other so-called blessings of civilization have anything to do with happiness. You can be unhappy in spite

Mr Smith opened the discussion by saying that the topic suggested for that day was: "Were past generations happier than we are today?"
Natalie immediately wanted to know how the group could be expected to discuss such a question since, after all, they had not lived in the past and could not possibly know what life had been like in the past.
Paul joined in by saying that he disagreed with Natalie. It was, he argued, only natural for human beings to ask themselves what life might have been like in the past, and to wonder whether their ancestors had been happier or less happy than they themselves were.
This gave rise to the comment: "Well roared, lion!" from Ruth. When Paul, in turn, told her not to be sarcastic, she pointed out that she was not being sarcastic at all; that, rather, these words were her way of expressing agreement. She added that, in fact, people knew a great deal about life in the past, and that the group really ought to discuss the question and do away with the myth of the "good old days".
To this, Paul added that their ancestors must indeed have had what he called "a rotten time", without running water, electricity, motorcars, and the National Health Service.
He had forgotten to mention radio, motion pictures, and television, as George was quick to remind him.
Natalie, however, argued that she was not sure that motorcars, television, motion pictures, and all the other "so-called" blessings of civilization had anything to do with happiness. She

of all the conveniences of modern life, can't you?

Ruth: That all sounds very nice and grown-up, but have you ever thought of what life must have been like with people living together in crowded houses, without sanitation, constantly threatened by war, epidemics, and disasters?

Mr Smith: The danger of war is still there, isn't it? For all we know, another terrible world war may break out at any time.

George: But wars are much less likely today than in the old days when every little king or prince or what have you could start a war on the slightest provocation or simply when he felt like it. Our modern statesmen are much more responsible than that and, of course, you have to be much more careful about starting a war, anyway, if it may lead to the destruction not only of the enemy, but also of your own country and, indeed, all mankind.

Natalie: George is an optimist.
George: Don't get personal!

Paul: Seriously though, I could well imagine that life was quieter and therefore somehow more harmonious in the past. What do you think, Mr Smith?

Mr Smith: You're quite right, Paul. Life tends to be rather hectic these days, people are often restless and erratic. The only aim most of them seem to have is to make as much money

maintained that people were often unhappy in spite of all the conveniences of modern life.

Ruth, while admitting that Natalie's remarks sounded "very nice and grown-up", wondered whether Natalie had ever considered what life must have been like with people living together in crowded houses, without sanitation, exposed to the constant threat of war, epidemics, and disasters.

Mr Smith reminded them at this point that the danger of war was still there and that for all they knew another terrible world war might break out at any time.

To this, George objected that wars were much less likely nowadays than in the old days when every little king or prince could start a war on the slightest provocation or simply when he felt like it. In his view, modern statesmen were much more responsible than that, and of course one had to be much more careful about starting a war, anyway, if it might lead to the destruction not only of the enemy, but also of one's own country and, indeed, all mankind.

These remarks of George's led to a clash between Natalie and George, she calling him an optimist, and he warning her not to get personal.

Paul, who spoke next, raised a new point by saying he could well imagine that life had been quieter and therefore somehow more harmonious in the past. He wanted to know what Mr Smith had to say about this.

Mr Smith replied that he agreed with Paul. Life tended to be rather hectic these days, he said, and people were often restless and erratic. The only aim most of them seemed to have was

The Tenses

as possible as quickly as possible.

Natalie: Quite. And just think of family life. Family ties are much looser nowadays, and the home no longer provides the security it used to. It's just a place where the family hastily meets to eat and to watch television.

Ruth: I agree. Family life isn't what it used to be. Still, even if I had the choice, I would rather live in the second half of the twentieth century than in Shakespeare's time or in the time of Alfred the Great.

Mr Smith: Well, I think we all agree on this point. Whatever advantages life in the past may have had, we feel we are now, on the whole, better off than our ancestors. Happiness, of course, is not an automatic result of prosperity and the hundred little amenities of modern life. And grateful though we are for the blessings of modern civilization, we should always be wise enough to seek happiness not in material values but in friendship, love, peace of mind, and, perhaps, a feeling of achievement.

to make as much money as possible as quickly as possible.
Natalie was in full agreement with Mr Smith's remarks and drew their attention to family life, saying that family ties were much looser nowadays, and that the home no longer provided the security it used to. The home, she said, was just a place where the family met to have their meals and to watch television.
Ruth, though agreeing that family life was not what it used to be, said that, given the choice, she would still prefer to live in the second half of the twentieth century rather than in Shakespeare's time or in the time of Alfred the Great.
Mr Smith answered he was sure that all the members of the group agreed on this point, adding that whatever advantages life in the past might have had, people felt they were now, on the whole, better off than their ancestors. But he reminded them that happiness, of course, was not an automatic result of prosperity and the hundred little amenities of modern life. He concluded the discussion by expressing the view that, grateful though they were for the blessings of modern civilization, they should always be wise enough to seek happiness not in material values but in friendship, love, peace of mind, and, perhaps, a feeling of achievement.

150 Turn the following into reported speech, using phrases from the list below to introduce the sentences.
She accused him, She asked him, He complimented me, He doubted, He inquired, He insisted, He invited me, He offered, He reminded us, He said, Cicero once said, A famous suffragette once said, He suggested, She urged him, He warned him, He wanted to know, He wondered.

1. "I wish I could find that photograph." 2. "We must put an end to this non-

The Tenses

sense." 3. "We're not quarrelling, mind you." 4. "Take a seat." 5. "How long will she stay?" 6. "Don't be ridiculous!" 7. "The Bible and the Church have been the greatest stumbling blocks in the way of women's emancipation." 8. "You're jealous." 9. "What time did you leave the house?" 10. "Would you like a cigarette?" 11. "You should buy the red dress." 12. "May I stay, sir, for a moment?" 13. "They talk to each other once in a while." 14. "It probably won't be much use to you." 15. "Don't try to double-cross me." 16. "The exception proves the rule." 17. "I talked to her yesterday." 18. "I hope I never see any of you again." 19. "The customer is always right." 20. "Have you hurt yourself?" 21. "You've done a wonderful job." 22. "Will you still love me when you hear what I've got to say?" 23. "I can lend you the money." 24. "Bill, promise me that you'll never lie to me again." 25. "Please don't hold that lamp so low." 26. "A happy life consists in tranquillity of mind." 27. "Experience is the mother of wisdom." 28. "Let's have the next meeting on a Saturday."

The Auxiliaries

151 *Have.* – Sentences for observation.

1. He *has* written a letter.
2. My mother *has (got)* to wear glasses.
3. They *have (got)* a large house.
4. a) She *has* lunch at one.
   b) We *had* a letter this morning.
   c) We *had* trouble with the car.
   d) We *had* a good time in France last year.
5. I *had* a tooth taken out yesterday.
6. We often *had* him drop in of an evening.
7. I *had* him copy the exercise twice.
8. He *has* a friend waiting to see him.
9. His misfortunes *had* everyone feeling sorry for him.
10. He *had* a look at his new book.

152 Put the sentences under **151** into the negative and interrogative.

153 Compare the following.

1. a) He *hasn't (got)* a job now.
   b) He usually *doesn't have* a job at this time of the year.
2. a) He *hadn't (got)* a job last year.
   b) He *didn't have* a job last year.
3. a) *Have* you *(got)* to get up at six tomorrow?
   b) *Do* you *have* to get up at six every morning?
4. a) You *have* a large house in the country, *haven't you*?
   b) Every police court *has* two magistrates, *doesn't it*?
5. a) Who *has* a large house in the country? – He *has*.
   b) Who *had* a letter from England yesterday? – We *did*.
6. a) Who *has (got)* to get up at six tomorrow? – We *have*.
   b) Who *has* to get up at six every morning? – We *do*.

154 Put the following sentences into the negative and interrogative.

1. He has two children by this marriage. 2. They have their windows cleaned every week. 3. She has to give a lot of notice if she wants to claim free time. 4. He always has a gun on him. 5. I have to get back to London very soon. 6. We had a good holiday at the seaside. 7. We had lunch together yesterday. 8. She has someone staying with her. 9. I have to report to him every day. 10. We had our bathroom repainted. 11. He had to go there after all. 12. They have enough time every weekend to get a thorough rest.

The Auxiliaries

155 Insert the correct form of *have,* adding *got* where possible and making any necessary adjustments.

1. They ..... a party tonight. – That's nothing new. They ..... parties all the time. 2. You ..... the same trouble with your car yesterday? 3. You ..... any spare copies today? – We usually ..... some. But I'm afraid we ..... any today. 4. He ..... no chance of being elected. 5. You ..... a cigarette for me? – I'm afraid not. We don't smoke. So we never ..... cigarettes in the house. 6. Sports cars always ..... radial tyres? 7. You ..... the money with you? 8. What's your excuse? – I not ..... an excuse. 9. We usually ..... a lot of snow in winter. 10. You ..... to fly to New York tomorrow?

156 Study the uses of *need* and *dare* in the following table.

	Auxiliary	Full verb
1. Positive:	–	He *needs to* ask them.
	–	He *dares to* ask them.
2. Negative:	He *needn't* ask them.	He *doesn't need to* ask them.
	He *daren't* ask them.	He *doesn't dare (to)* ask them.
3. Interrogative:	*Need* he ask them?	*Does* he *need to* ask them?
	Dare he ask them?	*Does* he *dare (to)* ask them?
4. Emphatic positive:	–	He '*does need to* ask them.
	–	He '*does dare to* ask them.

Note also the following:
This is the last group we *need* deal with.
That's all he *need* know.
That's all I *dare* hope.
I don't know whether he *dare* try.

157 Sentences for translation.

1. Er wagte es nicht, sich umzudrehen. 2. Wie können Sie es wagen, meine Briefe zu öffnen? 3. Es gibt nichts, was er nicht wagen würde. 4. Er wußte, daß es die Zeitungen nicht wagen würden, das zu drucken. 5. Ich wagte kaum zu atmen. 6. Wagen Sie ja nicht, mich daran zu hindern! 7. Brauchen Sie Geld? 8. Ich glaube, mehr brauchen Sie uns nicht zu sagen. 9. Das hätte wirklich nicht zu passieren brauchen. 10. Niemand braucht es zu erfahren. 11. Er glaubt, er braucht für sein Examen nicht zu arbeiten, aber ich bin sicher, daß er's nötig hat.

158 *Can.* – Sentences for observation.

1. a) *Can* I go now?
   b) Answer this question. Then you *can* go. You *can* sleep if you want.
   c) You *can't* just leave it here, it's litter.

The Auxiliaries

2. a) He *can* lift 200 pounds.
   b) He *can* read.
   c) He *can* come to the party tonight.
   d) He *can* forgive anything but that.
   e) He *can* accept defeat without complaining.
   f) This car *can* hold five persons.
   g) You *can* go from London to Glasgow without changing trains.
   h) You *can* walk for miles without meeting anyone.
   i) He *can* be quite nasty at times.
   j) We *can* reasonably conclude from this that such is the case.
   k) Only the House *can* originate financial measures.
3. I *can* show you the report if you like.
4. *Can* you tell me the right time, please?
5. What ˈ*can* he want?
6. I *can* see the stars.
7. *Can't* you leave him alone?
8. I wonder why she hasn't arrived yet. – Stop worrying about her. She *can* easily have forgotten that she was invited.

159 In which of the examples under **158** may *could* be used as a past tense of *can*?

160 *Could*. – Sentences for observation.

1. a) *Could* I go now?
   b) *Could* I come again tomorrow?
2. *Could* you look after the baby for a minute, please?
3. a) We *could* say you were staying in London.
   b) I *could* lift 200 pounds (if I tried).
4. It *could* be true, but I hardly think it is.
5. She had no idea what time it was. It *could* have been midnight.
6. She *could* have done it by now, but I'm afraid she forgot all about it.
7. We *could* have had lunch at twelve.

161 Fill in *could* or *was / were able to*.

1. I ..... discuss this with him when we met last Saturday. 2. Two windows in the courtyard were lit. In one she ..... see the flickering blue shadow of a television screen. 3. We used Ben's room as a studio. What else ..... we do? 4. Liz had some German, which she had learnt from her aunt, and she was surprised how quickly she ..... use it. 5. She wanted to run, but he held her so firmly that she ..... not. 6. She ..... call on us whenever she wanted to. 7. I ..... join the broken ends with glue yesterday. 8. We ..... finish our work by 10 o'clock. 9. I had no key, so I ..... not lock the door. 10. ..... you see

him before he left? 11. He ..... eat anything before he was ill. 12. They ..... catch the train because I drove them to the station.

May. – Sentences for observation. | 162

1. a) You *may* speak again later.
   b) Visitors *may* walk on the lawn.
   c) *May* I call on you again next week?
2. a) Please keep your voice down. We *may* be overheard.
   b) He *may* have been tipped off by someone.
   c) You *may* go from London to Glasgow without changing trains.
   d) You *may* walk for miles without meeting anyone.
3. a) *May* they all be damned.
   b) *May* the best man win.
4. He *may* be slow but he is thorough.
5. What *may* ¹he want?
6. We *may* as well go to the theatre tonight.

What are the negative forms of 1 a, b, c and 2 b, c, d in **162**? | 163

What are the interrogative forms of 2 a, b, c, d in **162**? | 164

May in subordinate clauses. – Sentences for observation. | 165

1. I beg that I *may* be allowed to continue.
2. I'm afraid we *may* lose our way.
3. A man like him flatters so that he *may* win favour.
4. Whatever he *may* say, I won't believe him.
5. I hope you *may* make a lot of money out of it.
6. It is possible that one of the bills *may* be passed.
7. He demands that a large sum *may* be put at his disposal.

Might. – Sentences for observation. | 166

1. *Might* I use your phone?
2. a) It *might* be a good idea to wait and see.
   b) He *might* make a lot of money out of it.
3. a) You *might* post these letters for me while you are out today.
   b) You *might* tell me the truth.
4. a) You *might* at least have apologized.
   b) But for his horn-rimmed glasses he *might* have been an efficient, not very well-fed courtier in a royal household.
5. Who *might* ¹you be?

The Auxiliaries

6. a) We *might* as well go to the pictures tonight.
   b) We *might* as well have gone to the pictures tonight.
7. She was tall and her arms and legs looked firm as if she *might* have been a swimmer.

167 Adapt the sentences under **165** so that *might* can be used instead of *may*.

168 Sentences for translation.

1. "Did you fly or come by sea?" – "We flew," Kiever said, "a very smooth flight." He *might have owned* the airline. 2. She guessed he was North Country, which he *might have been*, and rich, which he was not. 3. "How did you find prison?" he inquired. He *might have been asking* whether Leamas had enjoyed his holiday. 4. They walked to her flat through the rain and they *might have been walking* anywhere – Berlin, London, any town. 5. "If I want to dance, I know better places to do it." – Leamas *might not have been listening*.

169 *Can, could, may, might.* – Compare and distinguish.

1. a) It *may* rain tomorrow.
   b) It *might* rain tomorrow.
2. a) I *can* go and inquire.
   b) I *may* go and inquire.
3. a) It *cannot* be true.
   b) It *may* not be true.
4. a) Perhaps I *can* help you.
   b) Perhaps I *may* help you.
5. a) *Can* I help you?
   b) *May* I help you?
6. a) *May* I trouble you for a light?
   b) *Might* I trouble you for a light?
   c) *Can* I trouble you for a light?
   d) *Could* I trouble you for a light?
7. a) He *may* have been hurt.
   b) He *might* have been hurt.

170 Insert *can* or *may* as you think correct.

1. ..... I really trust you to keep your word? 2. Dreams ..... seem dreadfully real for a while after you wake up. 3. You ..... not believe me, but it happens to be true. 4. Nothing more ..... happen to him, I promise you. 5. You ..... be able to get away with assassination in the Balkans, but not in London. 6. ..... I have a word with Mrs Levy? 7. After you have heard what he's had to say, you ..... not feel quite so annoyed. 8. We ..... only give covering fire if they shoot. 9. That, if I ..... say so, is old hat. 10. You ..... go to any town in the world and hand over a piece of gold and get goods and services in return. 11. ..... I help you to cut the sandwiches? 12. ..... this be the last of your worries! 13. Beggars ..... not be choosers. 14. ..... you face all these difficulties? 15. Who knows, we ..... see each other quite often in future. 16. She ..... leave the court, but she ..... not go home until the hearing is finished. 17. ..... I come into your office tomorrow and talk it over with you? 18. What sense ..... a man make of his life?

The Auxiliaries

Put in *may* or *might*.   **171**

1. He did a bit of work in Boston, free-lance stuff. You ..... have met him. 2. "Did you," he asked – it ..... have been the most obvious of questions – "did you know he was going to hit the grocer?" 3. In an emergency it ..... simply be impossible to find a phone. 4. I ..... give Sam a ring later this evening. I think the sooner you two get together the better. 5. The police ..... want to question her. 6. ..... all his wishes come true! 7. It was dark. I couldn't see who it was. It ..... have been anybody. 8. I'll tell them, but it ..... be too late. 9. Mother, you ..... have let me know that you had plans to stay out last night. 10. I'll wait a week so that he ..... think it over. 11. You ..... give me a lift to the station. 12. Students ..... not bring textbooks into the examination room. 13. She was worried to death something dreadful ..... happen. 14. He's the sort of man who ..... do anything.

Will. – Sentences for observation.   **172**

1. a) Tomorrow morning I *will* wake up in this first-class hotel suite.
   b) They have not employed it and probably never *will*.
2. You *will* never regret it if you say yes.
3. a) You *will* do as I say.
   b) You *will* report to the principal at once.
4. a) I *will* lend you the book (if you need it).
   b) I *will* admit the very thought of staying with Irma is highly attractive.
   c) He says he *will* sign the contract now.
   d) I *will* go out and do a spot of shopping now.
   e) Mr Bond, I *will* pay you ten thousand dollars to stay here until you have discovered how this man Goldfinger beats me at cards.
   f) I *will* punish you if you don't behave properly.
   g) I *will* see him, even if I have to wait here all morning.
   h) If you *will* come tomorrow, I'll give you the necessary information.
5. a) *Will* all passengers please report to the Trans-America ticket counter.
   b) *Will* you dine with us on Sunday?
6. a) Oil *will* float on water.
   b) He has a quick temper and *will* get angry over nothing.
7. a) Three yards of cloth *will* make a skirt and a jacket.
   b) This *will* do if there is nothing better.
8. a) You *will* smoke all day, and then you complain about a sore throat.
   b) If you *will* act the fool, I can't help you.
9. a) That *will* be the milkman at the back door.
   b) I guess you*'ll* be saying to yourself, well, it's nice to see Junius Dupont again.

The Auxiliaries

173 *Would.* – Sentences for observation.

1. a) He *would* go out in spite of the doctor's orders.
   b) Regardless of warnings he *would* play with fire.
2. a) He *would* stand blows without blinking or shedding a tear.
   b) After supper she *would* talk to him, and he *would* lie on the divan, smoking.
3. Leamas tried to insist on paying his half. But Ashe *wouldn't* hear of it.
4. a) From his appearance he *would* be the one we were looking for.
   b) "I think," he said, "we will now take up your Ministry service in some detail. That *would* be from May 1951 to March 1961."
5. *Would* you please help us.
6. a) The explanation *would* seem to be simpler than we thought.
   b) The mechanics of transmitting the sound were perfect, I *would* say.
7. a) No stone *would* shatter that glass.
   b) The barrel *would* hold 20 gallons.
8. Parents *would* have their children do well.
9. a) I *would* like to recommend a series of articles.
   b) *Would* you care to stay with me for the weekend?
   c) *Would* you care for a glass of wine?
   d) *Would* you mind closing the window?
   e) He *would* rather (sooner) die than face them.
10. If only it *would* stop raining.
11. I *would* go today while the weather is pleasant.

174 *Would* in subordinate clauses. – Sentences for observation.

1. a) He kept on looking for the money that *would* solve his problems.
   b) He thought he *would* make a new start.
2. a) He could be helped if he *would* only do his part.
   b) If you *would* kindly wait a moment, I'll call the manager.
3. I wish you *would* not talk like that.
4. He stood there, dizzy with hunger, praying that the train *would* move.
5. He fixed broken glass on the wall so that the boys *wouldn't* climb over it.

175 *Shall.* – Sentences for observation.

1. a) I *shall* just put these papers together and send them off by the morning mail.
   b) I *shall* discuss the matter with my brother tomorrow.
   c) *Shall* you want to see me often?
   d) We *shall* hear evidence as we think fit.
2. a) You *shall* marry her, whether you love her or not.
   b) You *shall* be punished if you do it again.

The Auxiliaries

    c) He *shall* have the money tomorrow.
    d) He refuses to go? He *shall* go.
    e) It *shall* be unlawful for any person to keep any wild animal in captivity.
3. a) *Shall* I carry the box into the house for you?
    b) *Shall* my son drive you to the station?

Shall in subordinate clauses. – Sentences for observation.   **176**

1. He has promised that the work *shall* be done before Sunday.
2. He is determined that you *shall* obey him.
3. Criminal trials are to be held in public so that it *shall* be seen that justice is being done.

Shall versus *be to*. – Compare and distinguish.   **177**

1. a) We *shall* be married in May.
    b) We *are to* be married in May.
2. a) You *shall* proceed immediately to headquarters.
    b) You *are to* proceed immediately to headquarters.
3. a) He *shall* leave at eight o'clock.
    b) He *is to* leave at eight o'clock.
4. a) What *shall* I write?
    b) What *am* I *to* write?

Explain the following uses of *be to*.   **178**

1. Leave him alone. You *are to* leave him alone.
2. Many people *were to* lose their lives.
3. a) We *were to* have met at the theatre.
    b) He *was to* have given up smoking.

Insert *shall* or *will* as you think correct.   **179**

1. A capungo is a bandit who ..... kill for as little as forty pesos. 2. ..... all passengers proceed to gate number seven, please. 3. I promise you it ..... never happen again. 4. "Don't be cross, please," she said, "I ..... go, I promise I ..... 5. Listen, child, do you want to go home? Do as I tell you and you ..... 6. Mary and I ..... share the new flat. 7. For some perverse reason he ..... put his worst foot forward. 8. He ..... pay for the damage he has caused. 9. He has made up his mind that he ..... succeed this time. 10. The house with the green shutters ..... be theirs. 11. It is said that there are shops in London which ..... sell you books by the yard. 12. ..... he take your letters and post them for you? 13. I ..... not fill in this form. The questions are impertinent. 14. If you want me, there's an internal telephone to my room. I ..... be awake.

The Auxiliaries

15. Each candidate ..... be interviewed personally. 16. I have made up my mind to go, and go I ..... 17. It's very academic, but I ..... suggest it to my superiors. 18. What did you choose, if you ..... pardon the question?

180 *Should.* – Sentences for observation.

1. I *should* work if I had no money.
2. a) I'll put it through to CID when they come on duty. You *should* get the answer by lunchtime.
   b) It *should* be child's play for the three of us.
3. a) You *should* brush your teeth after each meal.
   b) Barton is a very hard man. We *shouldn't* forget that.
   c) Oh, but I *shouldn't* be telling you all this.
4. You *should* have known better than believe all those lies.
5. I *should* suggest that a guide to available materials is the first essential.
6. a) Why *should* anyone wish to do more than that respectable speed?
   b) Who *should* I see but my old friend Bob?

181 *Should* in subordinate clauses. – Sentences for observation.

1. I had expected that I *should* be able to make rapid progress.
2. a) If you *should* meet any old friends in the meantime, don't discuss this with them.
   b) They can easily be promoted *should* they wish it.
3. a) It's strange that they *should* remember the place.
   b) It doesn't seem logical that they *should* let me go.
   c) It was vital that Hawker *should* pick up the balls.
   d) I find it slightly ridiculous that you *should* be so indignant.
   e) It is expedient that one man *should* die for the benefit of many.
   f) I'm surprised that he *should* act so meanly.
4. He put a statement in the paper so that everyone *should* know what he had done.
5. She doesn't let him walk on his own in case he *should* get lost.
6. I propose that the case against Watson *should* be publicly heard.

182 *Should* in reported speech. – Sentences for observation.

1. a) I said, "I shall do it."
   b) I said I should do it.
2. a) He said, "I shall do it."
   b) He said he would do it.
3. a) He said, "I should do it."
   b) He said he should do it.

4. a) He said, "Where shall I be in 1984?"
   b) He wondered where he would be in 1984.
5. a) He said, "Where shall I go next?"
   b) He asked where he should go next.
6. a) He said, "My son shall apologize!"
   b) He said his son should apologize.
   c) He said his son was to apologize.

Insert *should* or *would* as you think correct.

|183|

1. For God's sake why ..... you care? 2. The rocks were icy and he was terrified lest he ..... slip. 3. I've been telling the committee that it is gravely underrated as a political weapon. – Christ, and you ....., too! 4. I do believe that young people ..... have a good time. 5. I wish someone ..... explain that to me. 6. I was telling my Davey to go there; he ..... not listen. 7. I knew that he ..... fall into the trap. 8. Why do you cover the mirrors? – So that we ..... not see our own grief. 9. Her eyes were deep blue against the light sunburnt skin and her mouth was bold and generous and ..... have a lovely smile. 10. They went to the cinema at 2.30, so they ..... be back here by 6.0. 11. I suggest he ..... take you back into his office. 12. It was decided that the matter ..... be referred to a special committee. 13. They spent that week walking in the hills. In the evenings they ..... return to the lodge, eat a bad meal and sit in front of the fire. 14. ..... you mind not interfering in my business? 15. I think it is better that she ..... find out what I'm like before rather than after. 16. Who ..... have foreseen this idealism in Sandy? 17. If you ..... kindly wait here a moment, I'll ring the manager's office. 18. It is essential that the matter ..... be kept out of the newspapers. 19. My God, the irony of it – that we ..... have given birth to a generation of office boys and clerks. 20. Where will he be now? – He ..... be there by now; the flight only takes an hour.

Put the following sentences into the negative and interrogative.

|184|

1. There *used to* be some trees in this field.
2. My father *used to* smoke a pipe.
3. They *used to* pay me every week.

Add question tags to the sentences in **184**.

|185|

Used to versus *would*. – Compare and distinguish.

|186|

1. "It *used to be* my flat," said Passmore.
2. She *used to be* married to old Paddy – Secretary for ... – I forget now.
3. He *used to smoke* fifty cigarettes a day.

The Auxiliaries

4. He *used to come* here a lot in the old days.
5. Occasionally she *would take* immense umbrage, such as when he hung his mackintosh on her peg.
6. He *would lie* on the bed, and she *would sit* beside him.

187 Insert *used to* or *would* as you think correct, making any necessary adjustments in word order.

1. I often think of how your mother ..... be when your father was alive. 2. What has happened? You ..... be a Socialist. 3. Yes, I still remember when you came back from school you always ..... go all over the house. 4. When alone, he remained faithful to these habits. He ..... even exaggerate them a little. 5. We ..... go to school together. 6. It was like midweek evensong when she ..... go to church – the same dutiful little group of lost faces. 7. Sometimes he thought of Liz. He ..... direct his mind towards her briefly like the shutter of a camera. 8. On paydays he ..... come back from lunch and find an envelope with his name misspelt on the outside. 9. She made the beef tea like her mother ....., in a glass with a teaspoon in to stop it cracking. 10. He was just like the characters in that book the college boy I dated a few times ..... read to me.

188 *Ought to.* – Sentences for observation.

1. We *ought to* follow the dictates of our conscience.
2. You *ought to* take care of yourself.
3. That *ought to* be the postman.
4. If you follow the instructions, it *oughtn't to* be too difficult.

189 *Must.* – Sentences for observation.

1. You *must* stop that noise.
2. You *must* come and visit us soon.
3. a) Man *must* eat to live.
   b) We *must* obey the rules.
4. If you *must* go, at least wait till the storm is over.
5. He *must* be out of his mind to say that.
6. He *must* have fallen had the railing not been there.

190 *Must* versus *should, need, ought to, have to,* and *be to.* – Sentences for observation.

1. a) They *must* sell their house.
   b) They *have (got) to* sell their house.
   c) They *are to* sell their house.

The Auxiliaries

   d) They *should* sell their house.
   e) They *ought to* sell their house.
2. a) They *don't have to* sell their house.
   b) They *haven't (got) to* sell their house.
   c) They *needn't* sell their house.
   d) They *don't need to* sell their house.
   e) They *mustn't* sell their house.
   f) They *shouldn't* sell their house.
   g) They *oughtn't to* sell their house.

Compare and distinguish. **191**

1. a) You *must* clean your boots.
   b) You *have to* clean your boots.
2. a) You *must* go now.
   b) What a pity you *have to* go now.
3. a) *Must* you get up early tomorrow?
   b) *Do you have to* get up early?
4. a) You *needn't* do it just now.
   b) You *don't have to (don't need to)* do it every time you see him.
5. a) *Must* I go, dad?
   b) *Need* I go, dad?
6. a) I *didn't need to* go.
   b) I *needn't have* gone.
7. a) I *was to* meet her at noon.
   b) I *was to have* met her at noon.

Können. – Sentences for translation. **192**

1. Der Bursche kann was. 2. Er kann nichts. 3. Der Junge kann sehr gut rechnen. 4. Er kann gut Englisch. 5. Er kann gut tanzen. 6. Sie kann nichts dafür, daß das passiert ist. 7. Ich kann nichts dafür. 8. Ich kann nichts dafür, daß ich dich liebe. 9. Was kann der Sigismund dafür, daß er so schön ist? 10. Kannst du mir Geld leihen? 11. Er ging vorbei, ohne daß ich mit ihm sprechen konnte. 12. Ich kann Pilze nicht vertragen. 13. Kannst du mir mal die Butter reichen? 14. Wer kein Blut sehen kann, sollte nicht Arzt werden. 15. Hier stehe ich, ich kann nicht anders, Gott helfe mir! 16. Er kann jetzt nicht mehr zurück. 17. Sie kann nicht mehr gerettet werden. 18. Die Kinder können jetzt nicht 'rein. 19. Sie kann einfach alles. – Kann sie kochen? 20. Ich kann nicht mehr. 21. Er kann Frauen nicht weinen sehen. 22. Wie können Sie es wagen, mir den Platz wegzunehmen? 23. Wenn er wütend wird, kann man ihn einfach nicht mehr halten. 24. Was kann schöner sein als eine glückliche Ehe? 25. Das kann ich auswendig. 26. Sie können sagen, was Sie wollen. Sie können mir nichts vormachen. 27. Das kann jedem passieren. 28. Er kann mit Kindern umgehen.

The Auxiliaries

29. Man kann nie wissen. 30. Ein Narr kann mehr Fragen stellen, als zehn Weise beantworten können. 31. Die Wand kann jeden Moment einstürzen. 32. Das hättest du mir auch vorher sagen können. 33. Du könntest mir ruhig mal helfen. 34. Er hätte sich ja denken können, daß wir abends nicht zu Hause sind. 35. Das konnte ich doch nicht wissen. 36. Er schrie so laut er konnte. 37. Das kann vorkommen, oder auch nicht. 38. Der Wagen stürzte in den See, aber der Fahrer konnte noch herauskommen. 39. Ich tue, was ich kann. 40. Bevor er krank wurde, konnte er alles essen.

193 *Dürfen.* – Sentences for translation.

1. Dürfte ich wohl mal kurz mit meinem Klienten sprechen? 2. Mein Name ist Eaves. Ich bin Polizeibeamter. Wenn ich mal kurz 'reinkommen dürfte? 3. Man darf nicht erwarten, auf dieser Welt Vollkommenheit zu finden. 4. Sie dürfen nicht über Sachen lachen, von denen Sie nichts verstehen. 5. Keiner darf herein. 6. Man darf erwarten, daß es ein toller Erfolg wird. 7. Er dürfte nicht vor zehn nach Hause kommen. 8. Das hättest du nicht sagen dürfen. 9. Man darf wohl annehmen, daß er Verständnis für Ihre Bedenken hat. 10. Es dürfte leicht sein, ihn zu überzeugen. 11. Man darf erwarten, daß alle einverstanden sind.

194 *Wollen.* – Sentences for translation.

1. Er will durchaus bleiben. 2. Was wollen Sie damit sagen? 3. Genau das wollte ich dich fragen. 4. Genau das wollte ich wissen. 5. Willst du etwa den ganzen Tag schlafen? 6. Er kann von mir denken, was er will. 7. Ich schicke deiner Mutter gern die Bücher, wenn du es willst. 8. Ich könnte ihn ruinieren, wenn ich nur wollte. 9. Wenn sie will, kann sie ganz nett sein. 10. Er will schon, aber sie nicht. 11. Er wollte aufstehen, konnte es aber nicht. 12. Ich weiß, was Sie sagen wollen. 13. Er will das gesehen haben. 14. Er will aus einer adligen Familie stammen, aber in Wahrheit stammt er aus den untersten Kreisen. 15. Wollen Sie, daß ich Ihnen etwas vorlüge? 16. Wollen wir jetzt gehen? 17. Ich will dir mal was sagen: Mach verrückt, wen du willst, aber nicht mich! 18. Wohin wollen Sie? 19. Er wollte sich nicht trösten lassen. 20. Er weiß, was er will. 21. Wollen Sie das bitte unterlassen! 22. Das will ich meinen. 23. Wenn Sie es durchaus wollen. 24. Wie es das Unglück wollte. 25. Das will ich gern glauben. 26. Ich wollte Sie nicht beleidigen. 27. Ich will nicht klagen. 28. Ich wollte, ich hätte es gewußt. 29. Er wollte lieber bleiben. 30. Sie wollen uns doch nicht schon verlassen? 31. Ich wollte Ihnen gerade schreiben. 32. Niemand wollte helfen. 33. Das will mir nicht einleuchten. 34. Es will mir nicht schmecken. 35. Wir wollen nicht darüber reden. 36. Das will viel sagen. 37. Das will überlegt sein. 38. Ich tat es, ohne es zu wollen. 39. Dem sei, wie ihm wolle. 40. Hier ist nichts zu wollen. 41. So Gott will. 42. Das will ich nicht gehört haben. 43. Was wollen Sie von mir? 44. Er mag es wollen oder nicht.

The Auxiliaries

45. Mach, was du willst! 46. Du hast es ja so gewollt. 47. Wie du willst. 48. Das will was heißen. 49. Das will nicht viel heißen. 50. Er wollte es einfach nicht tun. 51. Er wollte neben seiner Frau begraben sein. 52. Sie hatten nach München kommen wollen. 53. Wir wollen jetzt weitermachen. 54. Ich habe vergessen, was ich sagen wollte. 55. Er will mit Ihnen verwandt sein. 56. Er wollte mich schlagen.

Sollen. – Sentences for translation.

195

1. Was soll ich tun? 2. Soll man ihm glauben? 3. Es soll ihm ganz gut gehen. 4. Sie sollen gerettet worden sein. 5. Was soll ich? 6. Was soll das alles? 7. Er soll sich in acht nehmen. 8. Er soll die Finger davon lassen. 9. Ich möchte wissen, was das werden soll. 10. Er soll sich zum Teufel scheren. 11. Na ja, du sollst recht haben. 12. Der soll nur kommen. 13. Es soll nicht wieder vorkommen. 14. Sie sollte lieber nach Hause gehen. 15. Das sollte nur ein Scherz sein. 16. Du sollst nicht töten. 17. Er soll jetzt nach Hause kommen. 18. Niemand soll sagen, ich sei keine gute Hausfrau. 19. Das soll mich nicht stören. 20. Er soll jetzt sehr arm sein. 21. Warum sollte ich auch? 22. Sollte er es wirklich gewesen sein? 23. Man sollte annehmen, daß jeder vernünftige Mensch das tun würde. 24. Sollte es morgen regnen, dann können wir natürlich nicht schwimmen gehen. 25. Ich wußte nicht, ob ich lachen oder weinen sollte. 26. Es hat nicht sollen sein. 27. Viele Jahre sollten vergehen, bevor er seine Familie wiedersah. 28. Es soll nur ein Notbehelf sein. 29. Wer soll denn so was essen? 30. Was soll das? 31. Wie soll man sich da nicht ärgern? 32. Da soll sich einer auskennen! 33. Ich soll Sie von meiner Frau grüßen. 34. Damit soll gezeigt werden, daß man durchaus unschuldig verurteilt werden kann. 35. Das hier sollte für meine Frau sein. 36. Und das hier soll eine gute Übersetzung sein? 37. Soll ich dir etwas mitbringen? 38. Ich werde ihm sagen, er soll aufpassen. 39. Man tut nicht immer, was man sollte.

Müssen. – Sentences for translation.

196

1. Meiner Meinung nach hättest du ihm sagen müssen, was du vorhattest. 2. Das Buch müßte doch zu finden sein. 3. Wir freuen uns, daß Sie uns unverhofft besuchen, aber Sie müssen mit dem vorliebnehmen, was wir gerade haben. 4. Alle Menschen müssen sterben. 5. Sie müssen mich für sehr rücksichtslos halten. 6. Der Kerl muß völlig verrückt sein. 7. Ich muß ihn schon einmal irgendwo gesehen haben. 8. Da er blind ist, muß er sich beim Spazierengehen auf seinen treuen Hund verlassen. 9. Man muß sich beherrschen können. 10. Sie müssen mich „Sir" nennen; das ist die vorschriftsmäßige Anrede. 11. Herr Miller war ein kleiner untersetzter Mann, der aber in seiner Jugend sehr gutaussehend gewesen sein mußte. 12. Das mußte ja so kommen. 13. Der Staatsanwalt muß mich nicht verstanden haben. 14. So eine Politik mußte auf die Dauer scheitern. 15. Er muß nicht bei Verstand gewesen sein. 16. Sie können im voraus bezahlen,

The Auxiliaries

aber Sie müssen es nicht. 17. Mußten Sie die Getränke selbst bezahlen? 18. Wirst du die Strafe bezahlen? – Ich werd's wohl müssen. 19. Mußtest du mich unbedingt verraten? 20. Dieses unkluge Verhalten mußte ja ernste Folgen haben. 21. Wenn ich dich sehe, muß ich lachen. 22. Das mußten Sie doch wissen. 23. Sie muß immer das letzte Wort haben. 24. Man muß ihn sehr lange kennen, bevor man ihn richtig beurteilen kann. 25. Ich muß heute morgen zum Zahnarzt. Ich bin für elf Uhr bestellt. 26. Mußt du schon gehen? 27. Ausgerechnet an dem Tag, an dem ich Besuch erwartete, mußte mein Mann das Badezimmer streichen. 28. Ich erklärte meinem Sohn, daß er es lernen müsse, selbständig zu arbeiten. 29. Ich werde jetzt gehen müssen. 30. Ich habe noch was Geschäftliches zu erledigen und muß schnell zurück.

197 *Werden.* – Sentences for translation.

1. Als wir ankamen, wurde es gerade dunkel. 2. Sein Gesicht wurde rot, und seine Stimme wurde lauter. 3. Anscheinend ist er verrückt geworden. 4. Es war kalt und neblig geworden. 5. Sie wurde so bleich, daß er dachte, ihr würde übel. 6. Sie wurde kreideweiß, aber dann erholte sie sich schnell. 7. Sein Gesicht wurde einen Augenblick ernst, während er nachdachte. 8. Mein Mechaniker wurde krank, und ich mußte einen Vertreter suchen. 9. Ich werde wohl auch älter. 10. Sie sah, daß das Gesicht des Kranken blau wurde. 11. Es sah so aus, als ob er fast zu einem Einsiedler geworden war. 12. Er war plötzlich still geworden. 13. Du merkst wohl gar nicht, daß du langsam regelrecht widerwärtig wirst? 14. Bist du Anglikaner geworden? 15. Ich wurde so reizbar, daß meine Frau drohte, mich zu verlassen. 16. Ich werde jetzt gehen müssen. 17. Ich fürchte, mir wird schlecht. 18. Sie trank ihren Kaffee, der kalt geworden war, und verlangte die Rechnung. 19. Es wird ihm doch wohl nichts zugestoßen sein?

198 *Brauchen.* – Sentences for translation.

1. Niemand braucht zu hungern. 2. Sie hätten gar nicht so früh zu kommen brauchen. 3. Ich brauche Ihnen wohl kaum zu sagen, daß die Arbeit unter meiner persönlichen Aufsicht durchgeführt wurde. 4. Du brauchst mir das Geld noch nicht zu geben. 5. Man braucht mir nicht zu sagen, wann es Zeit ist zu gehen. 6. Man brauchte ihn nicht zu rufen. (= Er kam unaufgefordert.) 7. Du hättest mich wirklich nicht so anzulügen brauchen. 8. Ich gäbe viel darum, wenn ich nicht hinzugehen bräuchte. 9. Darauf braucht man nicht stolz zu sein.

199 Miscellaneous sentences for translation.

1. Das älteste der Kinder mochte fünfzehn Jahre alt sein. 2. Er sah immer noch jung aus, so daß die Mädchen meinten, er sei vielleicht noch nicht verheiratet. 3. Man könnte vielleicht irgendeinen Hinweis geben. 4. Ich dachte, du möchtest ihn vielleicht gern kennenlernen. 5. Ich dachte, du wüßtest vielleicht was, Lieb-

ling. 6. Ich könnte etwas Stärkeres als Wein vertragen. 7. Jeden Morgen gelobte sie sich: „Heute werde ich nicht die Nerven verlieren." 8. Ich bleibe nicht lange. 9. Kommen Sie doch 'rein! 10. Weshalb sollte ich in einer dieser albernen Quizveranstaltungen auftreten wollen? 11. Ich werde ihm nicht im Wege stehen. 12. Ich bin erst um acht Uhr frei. 13. Er war wütend und schlug vor, das Mädchen 'rauszuwerfen. 14. Es ist äußerst wichtig, daß er nicht erfährt, was passiert ist. 15. Es ist komisch, daß sie das gesagt hat. 16. Ich darf nicht vergessen, den Wecker auf halb sechs zu stellen. 17. Aber schließlich braucht das doch die Hochzeit nicht zu verzögern, oder doch? 18. Ich wagte kaum, mich hinzusetzen. 19. Wenn es doch nur aufhören wollte zu schneien! 20. Augenblick mal, wann war das wohl? 21. Selbstverständlich könnte er dir helfen, wenn er nur wollte. 22. Er glaubt, alle Frauen beten ihn an. – Das sieht ihm ähnlich. 23. Ich habe dem Verkehrsschutzmann aber tüchtig die Meinung gesagt. – Das sieht dir Esel ähnlich. 24. Zusammen dürften wir es gut schaffen. 25. Man sollte über die Fehler junger Schüler nicht lachen. 26. Was ist denn hier los? – Ach, was soll denn schon hier los sein? 27. Also, ich gehe über die Straße, und wen sehe ich? Meinen alten Freund Johnny. 28. Ich sagte dir doch, das Stück würde dir nicht gefallen. Aber du wolltest ja unbedingt mitkommen. 29. Früher hast du doch immer viel geraucht, nicht wahr? 30. Spielen Sie Tennis? – Früher mal, jetzt nicht mehr. 31. Liebling, wenn du nicht großen Wert darauf legst, heute abend auszugehen, dann möchte ich lieber zu Hause bleiben. 32. Es wäre besser, du bliebest zu Hause, bis deine Erkältung ganz vorbei ist. 33. Das hättest du ihm besser nicht erzählt. 34. Ich wäre besser gegangen, bevor er kam. 35. Ich wäre lieber vor einer Woche nach Hause gefahren.

Tags and short responses. – Study the following examples.

200

1. Positive statements[1]

    a) You're the forgiving sort, *aren't* you?
    b) We'll see each other again, *won't* we?
    c) After all it's Sunday tomorrow, *isn't* it?
    d) I'm your wife, *aren't* I?
    e) You *know* them, *don't* you?

2. Negative statements[1]

    a) I *couldn't* have something with gin, *could* I?
    b) There's *no* harm in writing a letter, *is* there?
    c) We *don't* know what will happen, *do* we?

---

[1] The tags in such sentences are said with *falling intonation* when no contradiction is expected, i.e. when the speaker is convinced of the truth of his statement and demands the hearer's agreement: ₁After ₁all it's ⟍Sunday to₁morrow, ⟍isn't it?
Tags said with a *rising intonation* express the speaker's uncertainty: You're ǀnot a⟍fraid, ⁄are you?

The Auxiliaries

d) I'*m not* wrong, *am* I?
e) You'*re not* afraid, *are* you?

3. Commands and requests¹

a) ˈCall again toˋmorrow, ˈ*will* you?
ˈCall again toᵛmorrow, ˋ*will* you?
b) ˈCall again toˋmorrow, ˈ*won't* you?
ˈCall again toᵛmorrow, ˋ*won't* you?
c) ˈCall again toˋmorrow, ˈ*would* you?
ˈCall again toᵛmorrow, ˋ*would* you?
d) ˈDon't come aˌgain toᵛmorrow, ˋ*will* you?
e) ˈLet's go for a ˋwalk, ˈ*shall* we?

201 Add appropriate tags to the following sentences.

1. We can't see it ourselves, ...? 2. We shall never know, ...? 3. I'll have to decide, ...? 4. I'm not going to die, ...? 5. Wonderful figure she's got, ...? 6. Let's have our drinks now, ...? 7. You'll give my apologies to her, ...? 8. He must be a most resourceful young man, ...? 9. You're very sure of yourself, ...? 10. You didn't waste much time, ...? 11. Bit chilly in here, ...? 12. We shall see each other from time to time, ...? 13. This is something worth waiting for, ...? 14. Light a cigarette for me, ..., darling? 15. We'll keep it from the boys, ...? 16. We must be patient, ...? 17. You love this place, ...? 18. You're not going to call on him, ...? 19. I'm a prisoner for life, ...? 20. Just wait a minute, ...? 21. Rita, I don't think you've ever met my mother, ...? 22. Let's look at the atlas, ...? 23. Well, in those old-fashioned regiments everyone was nice, ...? 24. Nothing holds their attention very long nowadays, ...? 25. I'm your father, ...? 26. Lend me a handkerchief, ...? 27. Comes as a surprise, ...? 28. There's been another murder, ...? 29. I'd better clear the way, sir, ...? 30. You don't seem to have any special interest in it, ...? 31. Wear a hat when you go up to the office, ...? 32. Then I can only believe that you've done what they say, ...? 33. I don't think you said it all in the letter, ...? 34. I can't do anything by myself, ...? 35. I'm terribly aggressive, ...? 36. I won't get wet then, ...? 37. So much has happened suddenly, ...? 38. No reason why I shouldn't, ...? 39. No need to bring that up, ...?

¹ The normal intonation patterns are indicated by means of tonetic stress marks. For explanatory details see Roger Kingdon, *The Groundwork of English Intonation*, London 1958.

The Auxiliaries

202 Comment on the tags in the following examples.¹

1. So she hates him, *does she*?
2. Oh, so she found you, *did she*?
3. This is your famous English fox hunting, *is it*?
4. Oh, he said that, *did he*?
5. I'm underrating your goodness, *am I*, darling?
6. So you don't like him, *don't you*?
7. So there's nobody in, *isn't there*?

203 Add tags in the same way as under **202**. Make sure you use a rising intonation on the tags.

1. So they're still shilly-shallying, ... ? 2. Oh, you know him, ... ? 3. Oh, you went to London first, ... ? 4. So he's going to divorce her, ... ? 5. I woke the wifey, ... ? Sorry. 6. Oh, he committed suicide, ... ? 7. So you can't help them, ... ? 8. Oh, that doesn't matter, ... ? 9. You want it on paper, ... ? 10. So you didn't tell anybody, ... ?

204 What is expressed by the following short responses?

He has gone to the pictures. – 1. Oh, ′has he?
2. Oh, ˋhas he?
3. ˋOh, he ˋhas, ′has he?
4. ˋYes, he ˋhas.
5. ˋYes, ˋhasn't he?
6. ˋYes, he ˋhas, ˋhasn't he?
7. ′So he ˎhas.
8. ˋNo, he ′hasn't.
9. ¡So have ˋthey.

205 Put the statement in **204** into the negative and supply the corresponding short answers.

206 Give appropriate translations for the following sentences.

1. Why did you go there? – *But I didn't*. 2. Why didn't you tell him the truth? – *But I did*. 3. Maybe I know more about that affair than you *do*. 4. Who broke that window? – *I did*. 5. We couldn't bear the heat on the beach. – *Neither could we*. 6. I like westerns, *don't you*? 7. You know everything better than anybody else *does*. 8. I go to London more often than you *do*. 9. "Have you

¹ These tags are all said with a rising intonation.

The Auxiliaries

made up your mind at last?" he asked. I told him I *had*. 10. I never knew anybody who appreciated a good joke as much as he *did*. 11. That's the third time you've torn your trousers this week, Johnny. You 'are a nuisance! 12. I *do* wonder why he suddenly gave her the go-by.

207 Sentences for translation.

1. Wir müssen jetzt gehen. Und du auch. 2. Du weißt genauso gut wie ich, wer der Täter war. 3. Seine Frau ist etwas älter als er. 4. So einem Dummkopf wie dir bin ich noch nie begegnet. 5. Ich begreife dich nicht mehr. Was ist denn bloß mit dir los? 6. Könntet ihr euch denn nicht an einem sichereren Ort treffen? 7. Warum haben Sie meinen Sohn geschlagen? – Aber ich habe ihn ja gar nicht geschlagen. 8. Mir hat es gefallen, und ihr auch. 9. Soll ich dir eine Tasse Tee machen, Papa? – Ach ja, bitte. 10. Es ist also doch wahr, daß er uns hintergangen hat. 11. Ich habe wirklich vorhin jemanden in dem Gebüsch da stöhnen gehört. 12. Wer hat denn diesen furchbaren Krach gemacht? – Wir. 13. Ich kann es nicht, und du kannst es auch nicht. 14. Erinnere mich doch bitte nachher daran, daß ich Herrn Miller anrufe. 15. Ich habe gehört, Sie sind im Examen durchgefallen. – Aber das stimmt ja gar nicht. 16. Hören Sie. Sie wollen doch sicher Ihre Familie wiedersehen. Tun Sie, was ich sage, und Sie werden sie wiedersehen. 17. Ich bin ebensowenig an einem Skandal interessiert wie Sie. 18. Wie kannst du bloß so über deine Freunde reden? 19. Harry ist letzten Sonntag nicht in die Kirche gegangen, und seine Schwester auch nicht. 20. Warum hast du dem Alten nicht geholfen? – Aber ich habe ihm doch geholfen. 21. Ich habe ihn wirklich nie leiden können. 22. Sie wird sicher überrascht sein, wenn sie das erfährt.

The Subjunctive

The subjunctive. – Sentences for observation. |208|

1. a) God *help* us!
   b) *May* God help us!
2. a) They insisted that I *come* out with them to the movies.
   b) They had insisted that the third landing *should* be made at Casablanca.
3. a) She was sorry there was no work here; she suggested that he *try* the Labour Exchange in the nearby town.
   b) I suggested that I *should* make another business trip for him.
4. a) He demanded that the other country *be* condemned and that it *give* up the fruits of aggression.
   b) The dictator demanded that the city *should* be defended to the last man.
5. a) They would be the first to urge that the programme *go* on.
   b) The commission strongly urged that present penalties on marijuana use *should* be eased.
6. a) I wish there *were* nothing more to say.
   b) I wish there *was* nothing more to say.
   c) I wish he *would* come in time.
7. a) If this rumour *be* true, everything is possible.
   b) If this rumour *is* true, everything is possible.
8. a) Unless he *be* caught in the act, it will be exceedingly difficult to trace the crime committed to any individual.
   b) Unless he *is* caught in the act, ...
9. He stared at her as if she *were* far away.
10. When he awoke, it was as though he *were* a feverish frightened ten-year-old.
11. a) Whether this rumour *be* true or not, we cannot remain here.
    b) Whether this rumour *is* true or not, we cannot remain here.
12. a) Though everyone *desert* you, I will not.
    b) Though everyone *deserts* you, I will not.
    c) Though everyone *may* desert you, I will not.
13. a) It was especially important that there *be* no outstanding areas of friction between the two governments.
    b) It is important that Mr Groves *should* be as fully informed as possible.

Sentences for translation. |209|

1. Nehmen wir einmal an, er wäre nicht zu Hause, was soll ich dann tun? 2. Es ist lächerlich, daß du dich von diesen blöden Kerlen um den kleinen Finger wikkeln läßt. 3. Es ist sehr natürlich, daß Sie ihn kennenlernen möchten. 4. Er bestand darauf, daß ich zu Bett ging, weil ich eine Erkältung hatte. 5. Ich schlage Herrn Peters vor, daß er mich morgen um neun dort trifft. 6. Bevor sich alle zurückzogen, wurde festgelegt, daß die ganze Gesellschaft am nächsten Tage hinüberfahre, um das Schloß zu besichtigen. 7. Er verlangte, daß das gesamte Gepäck vorausgeschickt werde. 8. Sie hatte gebetet, ihr Vater möge in Sicherheit sein und der Krieg möge bald vorüber sein. 9. Ich schlug Michael vor, einen Spa-

The Subjunctive

ziergang am Strand mit mir zu machen. 10. Es ist unbedingt erforderlich, daß eine Maschine geschickt wird, die ihn nach England fliegt. 11. Es ist unfair zu verlangen, daß eine Analogie vollständig sei bis in die kleinsten Einzelheiten. 12. Ich sage dir das alles nur, damit du verstehst, was ich zu tun beabsichtige. 13. Sei er auch noch so reich, Gesundheit und Zufriedenheit kann er sich nicht kaufen. 14. Das verhüte Gott! 15. Der Teufel soll ihn holen! 16. Wie dem auch sei, wir bleiben bei unserem Plan. 17. Ich wußte, daß, komme was da wolle, ich sie wieder besuchen würde. 18. Und wäre er mein eigener Sohn, ich würde ihn verurteilen. 19. Es ist wichtig, daß nichts in London passiert, was unsere Pläne umstoßen könnte. 20. Ich hatte große Angst, daß irgend etwas schiefgehen könnte. 21. Ihr Mann bat sie dringend, sie möge zu Hause bleiben. 22. Die Kommission empfiehlt, die Schülerzahl zu verringern. 23. „Ich verstehe nichts davon", sagte sie hastig, damit Edward nicht denke, sie wolle mit ihrem Wissen prahlen. 24. Es tut mir leid, daß Sie gezwungen sind, Ihren neuen Wagen wieder zu verkaufen. 25. Es ist unmöglich, daß sie mich so hintergangen hat. 26. Es ist mein Wunsch, daß das Land so bald wie möglich zu einer parlamentarischen Regierungsform zurückkehrt. 27. Es kam uns verdächtig vor, daß der Mann ein Gewehr bei sich hatte. 28. Vor einigen Jahren sagte mein Vater, er wünschte, ich wäre als kleines Kind gestorben. 29. Es ist schon ein merkwürdiger Zufall, daß wir uns in einem so gottverlassenen Nest wiedersehen. 30. Es ist Wahnsinn, daß zwei leiden, wenn nur einer verantwortlich ist.

Irregular Verbs

Provide the past-tense forms of the verbs in brackets.

210

1. In the middle of the night thunder (awake) Henry. 2. He (awake) after eight hours, conscious of pain and nausea. 3. I must have dozed off around four o'clock because I (wake) with a start, lying on the divan. 4. He (bet) me a dollar that he could beat me in each and every competition. 5. He thanked his friend and (bid) him good-bye. 6. They (bid) him enter. 7. They (bid) £25,000 and got the contract. 8. She (bid) frantically for the old chair. 9. They (breakfast) late, (go) to several bookshops, and at a quarter to one (meet) Honoria and her friend Anne Stirling. 10. Knitting had now become a mania with us. The use of the things we (knit) no longer mattered. The knitting itself was like a drug, a medicine. I felt, as I (knit), a restored womanliness... 11. She (knit) her brows. 12. The glow of the fire (light) her face. 13. He (light) a cigarette and went to a chair on the other side of the fireplace. 14. Her expression changed, and her eyes (light) as if with the glow of radiant memories. 15. Hundreds of candles (light) up the ballroom. 16. A scream (rend) the silence. 17. His boots (shine) with amazing lustre. 18. The policeman's torch (shine) on a dark heap in the road that had not been there thirty minutes earlier. 19. He (shine) his brass buttons with loving care. 20. As a child he had weak kidneys and (wet) the bed every night.

Provide the past-participle forms of the verbs in brackets.

211

1. It was as though she had been (waken) from a sweet dream by a clap of thunder. 2. I struggled up, feeling like a child (wake) in the middle of the night. 3. The three children had to be (wake), (wash), and (dress). 4. He trusted nobody who had ever (bear) arms. 5. She has never (bear) children. 6. Where were you (bear)? 7. You should have (beat) the stuffing out of him. 8. It was as though they had always been alone in a desert world (bereave) of people. 9. A large public fund was raised for the families made (bereave) by the disaster. 10. He had been (bid) to attend Sunday school, and he had disobeyed the order. 11. A German magazine has (bid) 250,000 dollars for his memoirs. 12. Life magazine seems to have (outbid) the competition for the memoirs that his daughter may write some day. 13. The General had just (broadcast) in the B.B.C.'s French Service. 14. I've got to get away or else I shall be (hang). 15. Have you (hang) up the lamps? 16. They didn't know where he had (hide) the stuff. 17. He was wearing a sweater that his grandmother had (knit). 18. His brow was (knit), his dark eyes watery, his mouth sagging. 19. His faded little face was (light) with rare triumph. 20. He had a (light) electric torch in his hand. 21. They had (light) upon the lonely spot quite by accident. 22. Fifty hostages were (mow) down in cold blood. 23. All this can be (prove) by experiments. 24. It has been (prove) that at the age of seven most of us have reached the age of reason. 25. These tendencies and practices have been (prove) wrong. 26. The night was (rend) by brilliant lights. 27. Suddenly the dead stillness was

Irregular Verbs

(rend) by a shot. 28. The prisoners' heads were (shave). 29. He has (shave) off his beard. 30. Imports must be (cut), armed forces (shave), food rations (trim). 31. His buttons were freshly (shine). 32. They had (show) her a copy of the letter. 33. After that, the work was considerably (speed) up. 34. On November 7th word came that Eve had been (strike) with appendicitis. 35. I was (strike) for the first time with an awareness of the financial responsibilities I had acquired. 36. The house was twice (strike) by lightning. 37. The clock has just (strike) four. 38. The dog had (wet) the carpet. 39. The baby has (wet) its bed again.

The Passive

212 The passive. – Compare the following.

1. a) This boy beat the poor dog just now.
   b) The poor dog was beaten by this boy just now.
2. a) Someone has stolen my books.
   b) My books have been stolen.
3. a) I have said enough here on a subject which I shall treat more fully in a subsequent chapter.
   b) Enough has been said here on a subject which will be treated more fully in a subsequent chapter.
4. a) He spoke at great length and people asked him many questions.
   b) He spoke at great length and was asked many questions.

213 The passive. – Compare the following.

1. a) The house *is built*.
   b) The house *is being built*.
2. a) The window *was broken*.
   b) The window *got broken*.
3. a) The carpet *was worn*.
   b) The carpet *became worn* by the constant tramping of feet.

214 Put into the passive if possible.

1. His return created a sensation. 2. They run cheap trains to the seaside on Sundays. 3. The girl gave a cry. 4. He resembles my uncle. 5. They had dinner before they left. 6. My father's family did not like Aunt Dinah. 7. Every day they walked a few miles. 8. The children had a good laugh. 9. They offered the butler a reward. 10. They denied her admittance. 11. They bought me a beer. 12. They found him a good wife. 13. My father gave me the money. 14. We brought them some food. 15. The party made him their leader. 16. The company appointed him a director. 17. Everybody laughed at him. 18. She had not slept in her bed. 19. They settled the account with the manager. 20. Somebody has tampered with my manuscript. 21. My father is looking after the garden. 22. They explained everything to me. 23. Nobody has ever spoken to me like this in all my days. 24. We could rely on the target-indicator flares to burn for some four minutes each. 25. He travelled with her. 26. Someone has been sitting on my hat. 27. You must send for the doctor at once. 28. We should go into this more thoroughly. 29. They took no notice of him, but they made much of his sister. 30. My parents will take good care of her. 31. At last they lost sight of the fugitive. 32. We must put a stop to it. 33. They took advantage of us.

The Passive

215 Sentences for translation.

1. Das Holz läßt sich leicht sägen. 2. Reife Apfelsinen lassen sich gut schälen. 3. Dieser Stoff trägt sich gut. 4. Dieses Buch verkauft sich gut. 5. Viele Dinge lassen sich überhaupt nicht übersetzen. 6. Der Deckel läßt sich abstreifen. 7. Das Buch liest sich gut. 8. Der Hut flog mir vom Kopf. 9. Ich wollte gerne den Film *Destination Moon* sehen, der in einem der großen Kinos am Leicester Square gespielt wurde.

216 Sentences for translation.

1. Man hatte sich bereits der öffentlichen Gebäude bemächtigt. 2. Man verliert diesen Punkt oft aus dem Auge. 3. Man muß an diesen Männern einfach ein Exempel statuieren. 4. Aber bereits auf dem Bahnhof hatte man sich des Ausreißers bemächtigt. 5. Man näherte sich ihm mit allen äußeren Zeichen der Verehrung. 6. Man kann sich auf sein Wort verlassen. 7. Man nahm allgemein an, daß es zwischen Frankreich und Spanien zu einer Absprache gekommen war. 8. Dort bot man ihm das Vierfache des früheren Preises. 9. Man zeigte uns die Sehenswürdigkeiten der Stadt. 10. Man hatte den Brief an Henry adressiert. 11. Man erklärte ihnen den Gebrauch der Maschinen. 12. Man muß mich vergessen haben. 13. Man hat ihm einen besseren Posten angeboten. 14. Man wies uns unser Schlafzimmer zu.

217 Sentences for translation.

1. Es wird hier stets viel getanzt. 2. Es wurde heiß gekämpft. 3. Es wird dadurch nichts gewonnen. 4. Es wurde mir mitgeteilt, ich könne künftig zu Hause bleiben. 5. Es war ihm eine große Belohnung versprochen worden. 6. Es wurde zwar lange über ihn gelacht und geredet, aber bestraft worden ist er niemals. 7. Es wurde berichtet, daß alle Kisten mit Whisky bereits gestohlen worden waren. 8. Es wurde beschlossen, den Bürgermeister zu verhaften. 9. Es wurde erzählt, der Inspektor sei bereits unterwegs. 10. In Deutschland wird jetzt auch schon viel Haschisch geraucht. 11. Wann wird hier gefrühstückt? 12. Hier wird nichts gestohlen. Sie können unbesorgt sein. 13. Dem ersten Angriff wurde noch tapfer Widerstand geleistet. 14. In dieser Kirche wird seit hundert Jahren gepredigt. 15. Mir wurde zu verstehen gegeben, daß meine Anwesenheit nicht länger erwünscht sei. 16. Hier wurde den beiden Herren eine glänzende Gelegenheit geboten, ihre Geschicklichkeit zu beweisen.

218 Sentences for translation.

1. Ein Stein verletzte ihn. 2. Es geschieht ihnen Unrecht. 3. Keine der anwesenden Damen nahm von dem jungen Dichter auch nur Notiz. 4. Der Präsident stellte der Zuhörerschaft den Sprecher des Tages vor. 5. Unsere Mannschaft wurde entscheidend geschlagen. 6. Weißt du schon, daß Ella geheiratet hat?

The Passive

7. Mir wurde die Aktentasche aus dem Wagen gestohlen. 8. Als er das Telegramm erhielt, eilte er sofort zum Krankenhaus, doch der diensttuende Arzt hinderte ihn daran, das Zimmer seines Vaters zu betreten. 9. Während der Auseinandersetzung wurde ihm die Nase eingeschlagen. 10. Auf dem Rückweg zu meinem Hotel hatte ich den Eindruck, daß mir jemand folgte.

The Genitive

219 The genitive. – Sentences for observation.

1. The road climbed straight and wide toward the *mountain's* round top.
2. All he could see for a moment was the *road's* new, black surface.
3. He sat there listening to the *stream's* toneless tune.
4. The *sun's* warmth seemed to bore into him.
5. It's something that really catches the *public's* eye.
6. Oil was the fountain of *Trinidad's* prosperity.
7. Look around and read great *Nature's* open book.
8. I did it for *safety's* sake.
9. He remembered an excellent little French restaurant less than a *stone's* throw away.
10. We had a few *minutes'* chat about things in general.
11. This was *Rosa's father's* Sunday afternoon, and he had been spending it as he always did, in his armchair by the fire with the News of the World on his knee, fast asleep.
12. Peter Catesby – that was *the young man with the sports car's* name.
13. It's not mine. It's my *landlady's daughter's*.

220 Supply what you consider to be the correct form of the word in brackets, pointing out cases which, in your opinion, admit of more than one correct solution.

1. The (barber) shop was quite crowded. 2. I'm due at the (hairdresser). 3. I heard such a funny thing at the (hairdresser) today. 4. She had just been to the (hairdresser) by the smell of shampoo, and a certain flush about the face. 5. She bought this hat at (Peter Robinson). 6. There's a newspaper seller outside (Woolworth). 7. Aunt Dinah was not actually an aunt: she was some kind of relation of my (mother). 8. This old lady was some kind of relative of Uncle Nick's (landlady). 9. Aren't you a friend of (Mr Leslie Dunright)? 10. I'm a friend of (Mrs Winter). 11. The old man had been a friend of her (father). 12. The matron of Macdonald Street Maternity Hospital is a friend of my (sister). 13. They're good friends of (Mr Hawke). 14. They're friends of my (parents). 15. I've always been a great admirer of your (uncle). 16. (Davies) have three schools of English. 17. (Robinsons) have developed special inks. 18. I bought it at (Smith), the (grocer). 19. The (stationer) will be shut, I'm afraid. 20. He was a patient of (Dr White).

221 Sentences for translation.

1. Die Frau meines Bruders heißt Sonja. 2. Ein paar Dummköpfe haben das Präparat trotz der Warnung der Kommission gebraucht. 3. Ich zweifle nicht einen Augenblick daran. 4. Ich wurde auf einen Artikel in der Zeitung von vorgestern aufmerksam. 5. Ich bin ein Freund von Joe Miller. 6. Sagten Sie, Sie gehen heute zum Zahnarzt? 7. Er wurde zu einem Jahr Gefängnis wegen Diebstahl und Hehlerei verurteilt. 8. Ja, wessen Tochter sollte ich denn sonst sein?

The Genitive

9. Ich glaubte, sie sei die Frau eines anderen. 10. Ich wohne im Augenblick bei meiner Tante. 11. Ist er ein guter Freund von dir? – Nein, aber von meiner Mutter. 12. Sie sagten, sie seien Freunde meines Bruders. 13. Ich muß immer lachen über die dicke, rote Nase von deinem Großvater. 14. Nur der Tabakladen und der Zeitungsladen in der Fortress Road waren geöffnet.

Number Form of Nouns

222 Supply what you consider to be the correct form of the word in brackets.

1. I weigh over two hundred and twenty pounds – sixteen (stone). 2. David Miller weighed fourteen (stone). 3. The buttress is five (foot) thick. 4. He's a big man, huge, about six (foot) six. 5. The missile is about forty (foot) long from base to cone. 6. You must have spent hundreds! – No, just a few (quid). 7. He chewed three (aspirin) and swallowed them dry. 8. There don't seem to be many (fish) here. 9. He caught three more (fish), the last a two-pounder. 10. He came home with a basket of eight (trout). 11. Although the water is cold and almost always covered with ice, it has in it enough (lobster), (fish), (seal), (walrus), (whale), and even some (species) of (shark). 12. There were two startled (deer) in the foreground of the picture. 13. On the coasts there are many (water bird), (reindeer), (musk ox), and (polar bear). 14. Those who did come upon (beast of prey) and survived the meeting found that the animals seemed almost as frightened as they were. 15. One winter they lost several (hundred) (head) of (sheep) in a blizzard. 16. The night fighters had shot down forty (aircraft). 17. All (spacecraft) have their own personal quirks. 18. She was now a girl with two (betrothed). 19. Three wooden (gallows) stood in the centre of the large chamber. 20. The publisher still believed that several of his authors were undiscovered (genius).

223 Choose what you consider to be the correct form.

1. It was a (sixteen-mile, sixteen-miles) walk over asphalt. 2. Many (aircraft, aircrafts) were troubled by icing. 3. I had reliable (information, informations). 4. Three (quid, quids) – that isn't much. 5. We worked for three hours in that (barrack, barracks). 6. Some elderly people speak of their own (death, deaths) almost with indifference. 7. Through the windows they could see a lighted (barrack, barracks). 8. A (gallow, gallows) was built. 9. It was a corner house at a (crossroad, crossroads). 10. What we want is a (headquarter, headquarters). 11. I opened the window and threw a small handful of (ash, ashes) out into the wind. 12. (Sport, Sports) (has, have) always bored me. 13. You are a damned old (soberside, sobersides)! 14. He told me about his army (experience, experiences). 15. Is it any wonder the poor boy steals when you pay him (a wage, wages) I'd be ashamed to give to a washerwoman? 16. I prefer the queues of Kensington to the sunlit (sand, sands) of the Côte d'Azur. 17. The Bible is a book composed of two parts commonly called the Old and New (Testament, Testaments). 18. There were several foul little trays containing tobacco (ash, ashes). 19. Both master bombers stayed over the target area throughout the (twenty-minute, twenty-minutes) duration of the attack. 20. With a wave the soldiers turned on their (heel, heels) and were gone.

224 Sentences for translation.

1. Seine Wohnung befand sich in einer häßlichen alten Gasse. 2. Hast du meine Brille gesehen? Ich muß sie irgendwo im Wohnzimmer gelassen haben. 3. Als

Number Form of Nouns

der Inhalt des Pakets überprüft wurde, stellte sich heraus, daß zwei Warenposten fehlten. 4. Seine Englischkenntnisse sind recht dürftig, aber immerhin hat er einige Fortschritte gemacht. 5. Seine Hose war ziemlich fadenscheinig; er hatte sie jahrelang getragen und es nie für nötig befunden, sich eine neue anzuschaffen. 6. Beim Umzug wurden ein paar Möbel beschädigt. 7. Die wertvollen Waren aus dem Osten wurden nach Konstantinopel gebracht. 8. Der Berufssport kommt durch häufige Skandale in Mißkredit. 9. Die Auskünfte, die wir erhielten, erwiesen sich als falsch. 10. Die Möbel sind alt, aber sie werden noch fünf Jahre halten. 11. Das Protokoll der letzten Sitzung wurde verlesen und genehmigt. 12. Hier ist eine interessante Nachricht für dich. 13. Dieses Grundstück am Rande der Stadt wird schon seit langem zum Verkauf angeboten. 14. Eine Schere kann zu einer gefährlichen Waffe werden. 15. Die zahlreichen und zuverlässigen Beweise, die wir jetzt in Händen haben, führen zu der Überzeugung, daß er das Verbrechen begangen hat. 16. Der Außenminister erklärt, daß die nationalen Ausgaben jetzt beträchtlich herabgesetzt werden. 17. Straßenkehricht wird oft als Dünger gebraucht. 18. Darf ich dir einen guten Rat geben? 19. Ich will keinesfalls die Beweise noch einmal überprüfen und damit die Zeit des Gerichtes verschwenden. 20. Glauben Sie, daß er sich darüber Gewissensbisse macht?

Concord

225 Choose the correct form, pointing out cases where either form would be possible.

1. The audience (was, were) large. 2. The audience (has, have) now returned and (is, are) taking (its, their) seats. 3. The audience (was, were) getting used to his way of playing the part. 4. The audience roused (itself, themselves) into applause. 5. The family (is, are) proud of (its, their) heritage. 6. His family (was, were) delighted to hear the news. 7. Jim's family (was, were) of about the same social status as my own. 8. His family, (who, which) (seems, seem) to have been perfectly decent, emigrated to Canada. 9. England (is, are) a nation of shopkeepers. 10. England (was, were) soccer champions of the world. 11. The Foreign Office (is, are) a government department. 12. The Foreign Office (is, are) being very sticky about passports. 13. The Government (has, have) accepted the Russian proposals. 14. The Government (has, have) discussed the matter for a long time. 15. The Government (takes, take) most of what I earn. 16. The Government (itself, themselves) (needs, need) to look again at the psychology of (its, their) handling of these negotiations and (its, their) relations with Rhodesia. 17. The Peruvian Government (was, were) taking no steps to punish adequately those responsible for such appalling atrocities. 18. A small staff of servants (takes, take) care of the house. 19. Station staff in the Southern Region of British Rail (has, have) been having lessons from a B.B.C. man on how to make announcements over (its, their) loudspeaker systems. 20. The Air Staff (was, were) by the beginning of 1945 anxious about the amount of direct army support being demanded of the bomber forces. 21. The whole staff, from the manager down to the office boys, (was, were) working twenty-one hours a day.

226 Choose the correct form, pointing out cases where either form would be possible.

1. The choir (was, were) at (its, their) best last Sunday. 2. The choir will not wear (its, their) vestments today. 3. The chorus (was, were) given (its, their) costumes. 4. The committee (has, have) filed (its, their) report. 5. I shall have to consult the committee, but no doubt (it, they) will agree with my suggestion. 6. The committee (has, have) been unable to agree on a place for (its, their) meetings. 7. The ill-assorted couple (was, were) married on 27 June 1949. 8. The couple (was, were) still standing there as she passed. 9. After six months the couple (was, were) happily reunited. 10. The crew (is, are) ashore. 11. The enemy (is, are) massing here for another major assault. 12. In twos and threes the enemy (was, were) creeping up the hill. 13. The class (has, have) been dismissed. 14. The class (was, were) divided on the question. 15. The team (has, have) deserved (its, their) victory. 16. The team played in (its, their) travelling costumes. 17. You don't think the Church of England (is, are) Calvinist, do you? 18. The Ministry (is, are) actually cutting down staff. 19. (Do, Does) the Press know? 20. Parliament (is, are) now sitting. 21. Parliament (differs, differ) over the question of war. 22. The congregation (is, are) coming out of the church. 23. The Board (was, were) preparing to fight a rearguard action. 24. The jury (was, were) divided in (its, their) opinion. 25. The jury selected

Concord

(its, their) foreman. 26. The public (has, have) taken motion pictures to (its, their) heart. 27. The English public (is, are) no fools. 28. The public (wants, want) more action and less words. 29. There (was, were) no royalty present at the première. 30. The majority (was, were) in favour of the proposal. 31. The majority (is, are) going home.

Choose the correct form, pointing out cases where either form would be possible. | **227**

1. The military (is, are) very much to blame. 2. For the moment it (was, were) the military (which, who) (was, were) giving all the orders. 3. The military (has, have) taken complete control of the government. 4. The Prussian nobility (has, have) never been rich. 5. The English gentry (has, have) never had the permanence of the Scottish landed families. 6. The Socialist party in New York (has, have) written to me to ask for a poetry reading. 7. There (comes, come) the rest of the party. 8. The local population (was, were) bitter and resentful. 9. The riffraff of Berlin (is, are) swarming round the quarter. 10. After a short adjournment the Crown (calls, call) the last prosecution witness. 11. The defence (has, have) decided to take another chance. 12. It is regrettable that the prosecution (has, have) condescended to make use of journalistic information. 13. Tottenham (was, were) at full strength to play Burnley at White Hart Lane. 14. Cambridge (has, have) won the Boat Race 55 times. 15. In the East India Dock Road the Salvation Army (was, were) holding a service. 16. The Yard (is, are) circulating a description at last. 17. The B.B.C. quite (understands, understand) the situation. 18. The R.A.F. (is, are) pounding hell out of the enemy's cities. 19. The Netherlands (is, are) a constitutional monarchy. 20. So far, the United States (has, have) never lost a war. 21. The Stars and Stripes (was, were) waving overhead. 22. The United Nations (was, were) formed in 1945. 23. The Philippines (is, are) a member of the Southeast Asia Treaty Organization. 24. New Hebrides (is, are) a chain of islands in the Pacific. 25. The clergy (is, are) violently opposed to this legislation. 26. Country folk (leads, lead) (a different life, different lives) from city folk. 27. Military personnel (is, are) not affected by these changes. 28. The police (is, are) making inquiries about the murder. 29. Meanwhile the police (was, were) getting to know her by sight. 30. The police (is, are) not very likely to interrogate him.

Choose the correct form, pointing out cases where either form would be possible. | **228**

1. The cattle (is, are) sleek and well-fed. 2. The vermin (is, are) an incessant torment. 3. Billiards (dates, date) back to about 1800. 4. Billiards (is, are) great fun. 5. The gallows (is, are) being erected at this very moment. 6. The gallows (was, were) right under the condemned man's window. 7. The gasworks (is, are) not far from the station. 8. The works (was, were) just under three miles from the city centre. 9. The news (was, were) becoming worse by the minute. 10. News (travels, travel) fast. 11. The summons (was, were) served by a grin-

Concord

ning bailiff. 12. The odds (is, are) no longer in our favour. 13. The odds (is, are) that he will do it. 14. What (is, are) the odds? 15. His wages (has, have) increased rapidly. 16. The wages of sin (is, are) death. 17. Postal savings (is, are) an anachronism. 18. His savings (was, were) confiscated. 19. All means (has, have) been tried. 20. His means (does, do) not justify his living on such an extravagant scale. 21. Every means (was, were) tried. 22. The only means of escape left to him (is, are) the Supreme Court.

229 Choose the correct form, pointing out cases where either form would be possible.

1. The barracks (is, are) crowded. 2. The barracks (was, were) a long low building. 3. His headquarters (was, were) in London. 4. The present headquarters of the United Nations (comprises, comprise) three inter-connected buildings and a library. 5. The headquarters of an organization (is, are) the place from which it is run. 6. His whereabouts (is, are) unknown. 7. Mary's whereabouts (was, were) very much on Allen's mind. 8. Acoustics (is, are) the science of sound. 9. The acoustics of this hall (is, are) excellent. 10. Acoustics (is, are) as important as any other technical aspect of modern construction. 11. The acoustics in the auditorium (was, were) poor. 12. Statistics (plays, play) an important part in the social sciences. 13. The statistics you gave us (doesn't, don't) seem to be very reliable. 14. The acrobatics he performed (was, were) really breathtaking. 15. Acrobatics (is, are) the art of an acrobat. 16. Athletics (is, are) his strong point. 17. Athletics (was, were) not one of his major interests. 18. At our college, athletics (is, are) performed vigorously and in many forms. 19. Economics (has, have) become a very complex field. 20. The economics of the situation (has, have) been discussed at some length. 21. Civics (includes, include) the study of state and national government. 22. Ethics (is, are) the science of morals, and morals (is, are) the practice of ethics. 23. Christian ethics (is, are) seldom found save in the philosophy of some unbeliever. 24. The ethics of the procedure (is, are) dubious. 25. His ethics in the case (was, were) questionable. 26. The bill comes to £58, if my mathematics (is, are) correct. 27. Mathematics (is, are) an important subject. 28. Physics (was, were) hard for me, although mathematics (was, were) always easy. 29. Tactics (is, are) the science and art of fighting battles. 30. The general's tactics (was, were) unobjectionable. 31. French politics (has, have) changed overnight. 32. Politics (is, are) a great field for the ambitious young man just out of college. 33. Politics (is, are) the noblest career that a man can choose. 34. My politics, like my religion, (is, are) my own private affair. 35. A woman's politics (is, are) the man she loves. 36. Dramatics (is, are) his hobby.

230 Choose the correct form, pointing out cases where either form would be possible.

1. Measles (is, are) a contagious disease. 2. Measles (is, are) contagious. 3. Although uncomfortable, mumps (is, are) rarely dangerous. 4. Shingles (is, are) a common virus infection. 5. Chilblains (is, are) extremely common in cold

weather. 6. Rabies (is, are) spread by the bite of infected animals. 7. Measles (is, are) not usually serious, but (it, they) can lead to complications. 8. Chickenpox (is, are) a mild fever which begins with the appearance of tiny blisters on the chest and back. 9. The modern bellows (consists, consist) of two flat boards. 10. The tidings (comes, come) too late. 11. Where (is, are) my scissors? 12. (This, These) hose (is, are) of the finest quality. 13. Great pains (is, are) being taken to make everyone as comfortable as possible in the circumstances. 14. At the edge of the field (was, were) the woods where I was to meet my friends.

Choose the correct form, pointing out cases where either form would be possible. **231**

1. Seventy-five thousand dollars (doesn't, don't) mean much to him. 2. Six years (is, are) a long time. 3. Ten miles (seems, seem) a very long distance when you have to walk (it, them). 4. Four quarts of oil (is, are) all the crankcase holds. 5. The first five years (was, were) the hardest. 6. Two more dollars (was, were) missing from the till this morning. 7. Three quarters of the surface of the earth (is, are) sea. 8. Three quarters of the bottles (was, were) broken. 9. What (is, are) £500 to a man like you? 10. Thirty thousand dollars (looks, look) big to a young writer. 11. Do you know how much money twenty-five hundred American dollars (is, are)? 12. There (is, are) two pounds ten in Granny's stocking. 13. (This, These) three pounds did in fact go to another post office. 14. Miss Burnham's funds, from all sources, (was, were) about one hundred and thirty-two pounds and sixpence. 15. There (was, were) still ten minutes before air time. 16. I don't think twenty-four hours (is, are) going to make any difference. 17. Three months here (has, have) made your English fairly fluent. 18. The last ten or twenty years (has, have) seen a considerable advance in the effectiveness of drugs to counter fear, agitation, and depression. 19. Four whiskies (is, are) rather a lot to have while waiting for someone. 20. World War II's sunken shipping represents a greater pollution source than the 118,000 tons of oil that (was, were) aboard the Torrey Canyon.

Choose the correct form, pointing out cases where either form would be possible. **232**

1. A number of accidents (was, were) fatal. 2. The number of fatal accidents (is, are) alarming. 3. A large number of new words (has, have) entered the language since 1940. 4. The number of things it was permissible to talk about (was, were) very small. 5. Nothing meant anything unless one cared, and the number of people who cared (was, were) desperately small. 6. Today, the vast majority of Catholic theologians (concedes, concede) that Luther was a profound spiritual thinker. 7. The vast majority of people (prefers, prefer) watching television to reading books. 8. It didn't take the Party more than twenty-four hours to get rid of (that, those) sort of books. 9. (This, These) sort of people (trades, trade) on idealists. 10. The number of pages assigned for translation (was, were) gradually increased to eight. 11. A number of people (has, have) asked the

Concord

same question. 12. Two thousand pounds' worth of pictures (was, were) destroyed. 13. Two-thirds of British industry (is, are) affected by this. 14. A total of 600 soldiers (is, are) here and (it, they) will stay a week. 15. A crowd of students (is, are) standing outside. 16. There (was, were) quite a large number of allied prisoners of war in Dresden. 17. There (was, were) such a multitude of things yet to be done.

233 Choose the correct form, pointing out cases where either form would be possible.

1. It (is, are) your neighbours that have spread this rumour. 2. It (is, are) always the young who are depressed at failure. 3. It (is, are) the spring mornings I remember best. 4. It (was, were) not only factories and power stations that were affected. 5. There was rustling of straw nearby and for a moment I thought it (was, were) mice. 6. He suddenly realized that he was drunk again. (Was, Were) it the three whiskies on an empty stomach, or was it her presence? 7. Now there (was, were) only whisky, bread, and some sausages left in their saddlebags. 8. I'm happiest when there (is, are) a high wind and heavy seas. 9. There (is, are) only two pounds of butter and a few packets of tea left. 10. There (is, are) eggs and bacon for breakfast. 11. There (was, were) an old bookcase, a small gas unit in a corner, pegs on a wall and door, two or three pictures, two easy chairs... 12. There (was, were) a double divan bed, several greasy armchairs, and a large table covered with dirty crockery and tubes of paint. 13. There (was, were) a few battered chairs and a table in the shack. 14. Even here there (was, were) furniture and pictures that any rich man would have been happy to possess. 15. There (was, were) a large pail of water, a mop, and a scrubbing brush. 16. As in every Churchill house there (is, are) a large library, and quarters for the secretaries. 17. There (was, were) tea, and there (was, were) bread and butter, and there (was, were) bread with currants in it, and there (was, were) buttered scones. 18. There (is, are) one Negro in the New York Philharmonic, one in the Cleveland Orchestra and three with the Pittsburgh Symphony. 19. There (was, were) no moon and no stars that night. 20. There (is, are) going to be some changes in this house. 21. There (was, were) no soap and no towel. 22. There (is, are) so many people in this life who just refuse to admit to their own goodness of heart. 23. There (is, are) a lot of offices in London. 24. There (was, were) an awful lot of mice around the place. 25. Neither you nor I (is, are) fated to stay here until the war is over. 26. Neither she nor her husband (knows, know) anything about it. 27. And then everyone retired to (his apartment, their apartments). 28. Everyone knew, everyone (was, were) sworn to secrecy, and everyone talked (his head, their heads) off. 29. She knew that everyone on the bus (was, were) straining (his, their) ears to hear every word that was spoken. 30. Everybody got up from (his seat, their seats) and took off (his hat, their hats). 31. Everybody seemed to be enjoying (himself, themselves). 32. Nobody likes being told (he is, they are) growing older. 33. No one in (his, their) wildest dreams (believes, believe) we can hold out against assault for more

than two or three days.   34. Willy is one of the few people in the world who (owns, own) a Churchill painting.   35. (Is, Are) Mr or Mrs Cowley in?   36. How (is, are) Margaret and the boy?   37. It struck him that his depression and boredom (was, were) probably due to hunger.   38. (Is, Are) Scotch oats on the breakfast menu?   39. Here (is, are) your cornflakes.

Choose the correct form, pointing out cases where either form would be possible.

234

1. All they had with them (was, were) a few cans of food and a completely sodden box of matches.   2. She said that everything Uncle Nick had ever told me (was, were) wicked lies, and I must forget it.   3. There (was, were) nothing but horses on the roads in those days.   4. What we have on our side (is, are) a few principles, a little integrity, a few decent aims.   5. The alarm signal (was, were) two knocks in case of danger.   6. The best feature of her face (was, were) her high cheekbones.   7. His preoccupation (was, were) women.   8. His remaining worry (was, were) taxes.   9. His speciality (is, are) murder cases.   10. The result (was, were) some bad days for Franco-German cooperation.   11. Odd jobs (is, are) my line.   12. Her main anxiety (was, were) her children.   13. My favourite fruit (is, are) apples.   14. The backbone of the army (is, are) still infantrymen.   15. The most unusual thing about him (was, were) his eyes.   16. Our chief trouble (was, were) the black flies that swarmed around us all during the trip.   17. Whisky and soda (has, have) always been my favourite drink.   18. The floor (was, were) bare boards.   19. Many a town and village (is, are) rejoicing tonight.   20. Up at Mrs Greevy's end (was, were) a tray with a very small teapot.   21. Most formidable (was, were) his posture, his voice, and his moustache.   22. Bacon and eggs (is, are) a favourite English breakfast dish.   23. Bread and water (is, are) no longer the typical diet for prisoners.   24. Your sister and brother (has, have) arrived.   25. The book (is, are) all lies.   26. The first thing we saw in the morning (was, were) two large rats sitting on the kitchen table.   27. The only thing you missed (was, were) the fireworks.   28. The next thing to consider (is, are) uniforms.

Gender

235 *Gender.* – Sentences for observation.

1. a) The fun-starved child revolted in the only way *he* could.
   b) "Oh no," the child replied, and *her* eyes lit up with happy anticipation.
   c) (Book title:) The Child: A Medical Guide to *Its* Care and Management.
   d) The most important thing about homework is that it is something the child should do by *himself*.
2. a) Ay, ay! as large as life; and missy played the hostess. What a conceited doll *it* is.
   b) What's the matter, sweet one? Is *it* worrying *itself* over that letter?
3. a) She had seen a man running through the woods and knew that *it* was Mortimer.
   b) I have never seen his wife; I only know that *she* is an Englishwoman.
4. a) Snuff, the brown spaniel, who had placed *herself* in front of him, jumped up for the expected caress.
   b) The horse still does almost all the things *it* used to do.
   c) The cold seems to take all the courage out of the thrush, while it puts the blackbird on *his* mettle.
   d) A parrot can talk like a man; *she* can repeat whole sentences.
   e) That fly has been bothering me all afternoon. I wish you would catch *him*.
5. a) A fishing boat got wrecked off the coast near here. Great seas swept over *her* and carried away *her* steering gear.
   b) This old steam locomotive is a real beauty, isn't *she*?
6. a) At such times Liberty must be saved by deeds, if *she* is to be saved at all.
   b) England has always been a sea power and *she* has never lacked defenders.

236 Choose what you consider to be the correct pronoun.

1. The moon was nearing (his, her, its) highest point. 2. The moon (himself, herself, itself) is not a particularly valuable piece of real estate. 3. The sun is apparently the largest and brightest of the naked-eye stars, but (he, she, it) is actually among the smallest and faintest. 4. The sun is shining in the sky, shining with all (his, her, its) might. 5. The decision was made to keep the boat in commission until (he, she, it) could be sold, and I was given the job of taking care of (him, her, it). 6. The big oak in front of the house was dropping (his, her, its) leaves. 7. Do you know that a submarine can outgun us on the surface if (he, she, it) wants? 8. When the submarine rests on the surface, (he, she, it) has the appearance of being longer than (he, she, it) really is. 9. The baby lay sleeping in (his, her, its) cot. 10. At the window a budgerigar fluttered nervously in (his, her, its) cage. 11. Because I could not stop for Death, (he, she, it) kindly stopped for me. (Emily Dickinson) 12. Even death has (his, her, its) funny side. 13. The Church has lost much of (his, her, its) influence in England. 14. The Church had begun to lose (his, her, its) hold on people who were no longer barbarians. 15. He passionately wanted Germany to have (his, her, its)

proper place in the sun.   16. Will Holland be able to defend (himself, herself, itself)?   17. Let us go the long way round, and show Mr Balintore how lovely Ireland can be when (he's, she's, it's) wearing (his, her, its) best clothes.   18. Mr Hoover remarked that Japan was six thousand miles away from the continental United States and that actual combat with (him, her, it) was even more improbable than with Germany.   19. We all long to help Russia in (his, her, its) agony.   20. Since white athletes are forbidden to compete against nonwhites, South Africa has had to cancel (his, her, its) long-standing rugby rivalry with New Zealand, which allows Maoris to play on (his, her, its) team.   21. The U.S. has reached a major turning point in (his, her, its) relations with Latin America.   22. Sooner or later, America would have to come in to save (his, her, its) neck.   23. Already Paris tossed restlessly under (his, her, its) occupiers' feet, anxious to cleanse the shame of the past four years, to find again (his, her, its) tradition of revolutions past.   24. Italy has to import most of (his, her, its) coal.   25. England was very much preoccupied with (his, her, its) own problems.   26. If a horse has a temperature, (he, she, it) must be inoculated at once.   27. Love begins playing (his, her, its) old tricks every spring.

The Definite Article

237 General – specific. – Fill in *the* where necessary.

1. ..... art never expresses anything but itself. 2. ..... nature is ..... art of God. 3. ..... conscience makes egoists of us all. 4. This crime will always weigh on ..... conscience of ..... man who committed it. 5. ..... death of the dog upset the boy. 6. One can survive everything nowadays except ..... death. 7. The road to ..... hell is paved with good intentions. 8. At that time nobody knew that six months later the country was to go through ..... hell of war. 9. ..... history of the world is but the biography of great men. 10. ..... history is the essence of innumerable biographies. 11. Australia is a continent where ..... rural life is predominant. 12. ..... conquest of ..... space is worth the risk of ..... life. 13. ..... literary life resembles ..... politics – at ..... bottom it is a contest of gifted men for popular favour and perhaps for a name in ..... history. 14. The difference between ..... literature and ..... journalism is that ..... journalism is unreadable and ..... literature is unread. 15. Dr Thompson will be lecturing on "..... Literature of the United States". 16. ..... love is like ..... war: easy to begin but very hard to stop. 17. There is no love sincerer than ..... love of food. 18. ..... man who makes no mistakes does not usually make anything. 19. ..... man is the only animal that blushes – or needs to. 20. ..... love of ..... money is the root of all ..... evil. 21. ..... scientists are learning a lot about ..... nature of ..... atom. 22. ..... nature arouses no response in me. 23. If you want ..... peace, you must prepare for ..... war. 24. He was arrested for being drunk and breaking ..... peace. 25. ..... judgment of this age must be left to ..... posterity. 26. We must learn to live in ..... society of people we don't like. 27. ..... truth is not always a comforting virtue. 28. ..... truth is the one thing that nobody will believe. 29. ..... civilized man cannot live without ..... electricity.

238 Idioms, collocations, etc. – Fill in *the* where necessary.

1. We will weigh ..... anchor at ..... dawn. 2. They knew at ..... bottom that they were only deceiving themselves. 3. At ..... bottom of his heart he welcomed the news. 4. I will give you the money on ..... condition that you spend it sensibly. 5. Under ..... cover of ..... darkness we climbed over the fence. 6. Under ..... cover of ..... fog, the boat slipped off to ..... sea. 7. This is the first time we've met in ..... flesh. 8. The castaways lived from ..... hand to ..... mouth. 9. The police now have the situation well in ..... hand. 10. He took ..... death of his wife very much to ..... heart. 11. He has always been a mathematician at ..... heart. 12. No one had ..... heart to tell him he was going to die. 13. The children were rather naughty at first, but I soon brought them to ..... heel. 14. What's the matter with you? You look very down in ..... mouth. 15. I'm completely out of ..... practice on ..... piano. 16. It's all right in ..... theory, but it'll never work in ..... practice.

17. You shouldn't wash your dirty linen in ..... public. 18. The problem isn't as easy as it seemed at ..... first sight. 19. One doesn't abandon ..... ship at the first bit of heavy weather. 20. It was impossible to retreat without losing ..... face. 21. Though he spent weeks at the task, he never once lost ..... heart. 22. His wife took him to ..... task for flirting with his secretary. 23. One shouldn't make ..... game of the weak and defenceless. 24. At the office he is ..... boss, but at home he plays ..... second fiddle. 25. If he doesn't win, he'll soon lose ..... interest in ..... game. 26. He thinks by all his fast talking and flattery he can pull ..... wool over my eyes. But he can't deceive me. 27. Once our counter-offensive has started, we shall soon put the enemy to ..... flight. 28. Certain advisers are under investigation for throwing ..... dust in the public's eye. 29. The sight of superior forces made the attackers turn ..... tail. 30. No one entering the house would now have grounds for suspecting that a fight to ..... death had recently taken place here. 31. Many people were put to ..... death for their religious beliefs.

Institutions. – Fill in *the* where necessary.

239

1. In Britain, ... executive power is exercised by the Prime Minister. 2. Every country has ..... government it deserves. 3. The object of ..... government in ..... peace and in ..... war is not ..... glory of ..... rulers or of ..... races, but ..... happiness of ..... common man. 4. ..... State and ..... Church are kept separate under our concept of ..... government. 5. The missionary went wherever ..... church sent him. 6. The best reason why ..... monarchy is a strong government is that it is an intelligible government. ..... mass of ..... mankind understand it. 7. ..... monarchy was restored in 1660 under Charles II. 8. In 1945 ..... Labour gained a majority in ..... Parliament. 9. In the nineteenth century, ... Parliament was made more representative, ... slavery was abolished in the colonies, and ..... legislation reflected the growing political and economic power of the middle class. 10. Bills are introduced, debated, and voted upon in ..... Congress.

Church, school, etc.; meals. – Fill in *the* where necessary.

240

1. He attends ..... church regularly. 2. I have never been in ..... church in Maddox Street. 3. He died in ..... hospital after an operation. 4. She immediately went to ..... hospital to see her husband. 5. The thieves were sent to ..... prison. 6. He left ..... school when he was fifteen. 7. His mother went to ..... school to see the headmaster. 8. John is still at ..... university. 9. ..... dinner was good, but I didn't enjoy the speeches that came after it. 10. She'll have ..... dinner ready in half an hour. 11. On the following morning I met him at ..... breakfast.

The Definite Article

241 Seasons and months. – Fill in *the* where necessary.

1. ..... spring makes everything young again except ..... man. 2. In ..... spring of 1965 I travelled extensively. 3. The farmer plants his seeds in ..... spring. 4. They returned from the States in ..... October of 1963. 5. ..... September had been lovely, and ..... October was not less so. 6. He had not seen them since ..... previous July. 7. Regular sport – tennis in ..... summer, skiing in ..... winter – had kept him robust and lithe. 8. At this time of ..... year, Nigeria is cold and wet. 9. It emerged that a great gap would be torn in their ranks early in ..... coming May. 10. In ..... May of that year, something totally unexpected happened. 11. I never eat at this time of ..... day.

242 Proper names. – Fill in *the* where necessary.

1. We spent our last holiday in ..... Argentine. 2. ..... Argentina remained neutral during most of World War II. 3. Many people who work in Manhattan commute from their homes in ..... Brooklyn or in ..... Bronx. 4. ..... Congo has vast mineral resources. 5. ..... Crimea is connected with the mainland by a narrow isthmus. 6. Only small sections of ..... Gobi comprise sandy or dune deserts. 7. ..... Lebanon is an agricultural nation. 8. The greater part of ..... Sudan is an immense plain. 9. Since 1955 Greece and ..... Turkey have been embroiled in a dispute over ..... Cyprus. 10. The climate of ..... Tyrol is bright and sunny. 11. ..... Ukraine is the richest republic of the Soviet Union. 12. ..... Ben Nevis in Scotland is the highest mountain in Britain. 13. ..... Jungfrau is a mountain in ..... Switzerland. 14. ..... Matterhorn was first scaled in 1865. 15. ..... Mount Everest is much higher than ..... Mont Blanc. 16. ..... Snowdon is the highest mountain in Wales. 17. The history of ..... Niagara Falls has been the subject of many studies. 18. He has written a fascinating book about ..... London of Elizabeth I. 19. ..... Venus is the planet closest to ..... Earth, and after ..... Sun and ..... Moon, the brightest object in our view. 20. ..... Fleet Street is the centre of ..... English journalism. 21. They watched him turn half right to cross ..... High Street. 22. They could see him walking towards ..... Kensington High Street. 23. His house is half a block from ..... Main Street. 24. He was walking down ..... main street towards the station. 25. We drove to ..... Palladian Club in ..... Pall Mall. 26. ..... Mall is a broad promenade in ..... St James's Park. 27. ..... Strand runs eastward from ..... Trafalgar Square. 28. The lights from ..... Albert Bridge wavered up from the dark. 29. He met her in ..... Victoria Park. 30. She decided to take a bus to ..... Bayswater Road. 31. The boat train from Dover arrives at ..... Victoria Station. 32. They had lunch in ..... Pennsylvania Station.

243 Proper names. – Fill in *the* where necessary.

1. Prices of admission at ..... Albert Hall vary considerably. 2. ..... Big Ben weighs more than thirteen tons. 3. His talk for ..... B.B.C. was recorded at

..... Broadcasting House. 4. ..... Mansion House is the official residence of the Lord Mayor. 5. Why don't you take the underground to ..... Mansion House? 6. A few yards away from ..... Marble Arch there is a small patch of ground called ..... Speakers' Corner. 7. ..... Marble Arch was designed in 1828 by John Nash. 8. ..... Rockefeller Centre has been called the Eighth Wonder of the World. 9. ..... St Paul's Cathedral is Wren's greatest monument.

244 Diseases. – Fill in *the* where necessary.

1. If you have ..... influenza, stay at home. 2. My brother has got ..... flu badly. 3. One of the children in ..... kindergarten has got ..... measles. 4. ..... measles is not usually serious, but it can lead to complications. 5. ..... mumps is in general a mild disease. 6. Don't go to ..... school if you have ..... mumps. 7. Don't go near John, he's got ..... whooping cough. 8. ..... whooping cough begins as an ordinary cold.

245 Miscellany. – Fill in *the* where necessary.

1. Babysitters are paid by ..... hour. 2. If he comes early, so much ..... better. 3. When he came back, he was definitely ..... worse for drink. 4. The story does not lose in ..... telling. 5. Go as far as the yellow building, then turn to ..... left. 6. He translated the book into ..... Russian. 7. The book was translated from ..... German by Eric Milne. 8. I can still remember the days when I danced ..... tango with her in ..... Normandy. 9. Is ..... polka often danced nowadays? 10. He plays ..... piano, and she plays ..... violin. 11. I frequently talk with Charles over ..... telephone. 12. We got the news by ..... radio. 13. She loves listening to ..... radio. 14. She loves watching ..... television. 15. We can't see the programme because ..... television is broken. 16. She decided to divorce him on ..... grounds of desertion. 17. When he awoke ..... next morning, he found that the footprints had disappeared. 18. Of the medical witnesses ten were of ..... opinion that the woman was poisoned. 19. Like most boys born on a farm, Mason was exceptionally sensitive to ..... weather.

246 Sentences for translation.

1. Reisende vom Kontinent kommen meistens an der Victoria Station an. 2. Ich mache meine Einkäufe nicht so besonders gern in der Oxford Street. 3. Das Guggenheim-Museum ist gegenüber vom Central Park. 4. Soweit ich mich erinnere, war es im März jenes Jahres. 5. Wir erreichten Aberdeen am folgenden Mittwoch und blieben dort den Sonntag über. 6. Ich werde das Abendbrot in einer halben Stunde fertig haben. 7. Nach dem Abendessen sieht er meistens fern. 8. Irgendwie gelang es ihr, ihm wenigstens Foxtrott beizubringen. 9. Die

The Definite Article

ersten Nahaufnahmen des Mars wurden im Juli 1965 gemacht. 10. Der Mond dreht sich um die Erde, und die Erde dreht sich um die Sonne. 11. Die Angel-Fälle in Venezuela sind zwanzigmal so hoch wie die Niagara-Fälle. 12. Leider gelang es den Dieben, im Schutz der Dunkelheit zu entkommen. 13. Bei allem, was er tat, war das Glück ihm stets hold. 14. Kaiser Wilhelm II. war bei den Engländern gar nicht beliebt. 15. Die Zeugen Jehovas sind eine äußerst aktive Religionsgemeinschaft. 16. Erst seit kurzem hat die Frau das Wahlrecht. 17. Zur Zeit der Romantik war die französische Literatur besonders einflußreich. 18. Die Nacht brach herein, ehe sie ihr Ziel erreichten.

The Indefinite Article

247 Fill in *a(n)* where necessary.

1. That's ..... good advice. 2. What ..... fine news! 3. I have never heard such ..... nonsense. 4. This book has ..... clear print. 5. The boy bears ..... strong resemblance to his father. 6. I can't think why he wanted to go out in such ..... weather. 7. What ..... wretched weather!

248 Fill in *a(n)* where necessary.

1. As ..... child, I often had nightmares. 2. Our food supplies are at ..... end. 3. By the time the meeting had come to ..... end, he was fast asleep. 4. The boy shows ..... interest in sports. 5. His insults made her fly into ..... passion and leave the room. 6. She flew into ..... temper when he told her she was wrong. 7. As ..... result of the accident he had to undergo four painful operations.

249 Fill in *a(n)* where necessary.

1. The long walk gave me ..... good appetite. 2. He is a man with ..... voracious appetite. 3. He was glad enough to have the soup, and he fell to with ..... appetite. 4. She ate with ..... appetite, but he did not. 5. He's got ..... birthday today. 6. Why on earth didn't you tell me you had ..... birthday on Sunday? 7. Do you catch ..... cold easily? 8. We'd only catch ..... cold in the draught. 9. He hoped he wasn't catching ..... cold. 10. You look as though you have ..... fever. 11. Some of the men had ..... fever, some ..... hookworm, and some had huge horny scabs on their arms. 12. You've still got ..... temperature, and getting up is out of the question. 13. He has ..... temperature of 101 degrees.

250 Fill in *a(n)* where necessary.

1. The sound of shooting threw the crowd into ..... panic. 2. There is always danger of ..... panic when a theatre catches fire. 3. He felt ..... sudden impatience when he saw what was happening. 4. Do you think that 30 years' imprisonment was ..... fair punishment for the train robbers? 5. At that time nobody knew that Baxter had turned ..... traitor. 6. She was always fresh and neat and had ..... excellent taste in clothes. 7. The furniture is quite new, but in ..... dreadful taste.

251 Fill in *a(n)* where necessary.

1. He lost ..... part of his fortune in the transaction. 2. A sense of humour is ..... part of a healthy personality. 3. His car was as much ..... part of him as his bed. 4. He felt himself to be ..... part of the team. 5. It was ..... quarter

The Indefinite Article

to three by his watch. 6. They talked awkwardly for ..... quarter of an hour until Jim, protesting tiredness, went sullenly to bed. 7. I hope you have ..... merry Christmas and a happy New Year. 8. ..... merry Christmas to you all!

252 Fill in *a(n)* where necessary.

1. When I spoke to him on the phone the following morning, he said he was in ..... dreadful condition, that his hangover was "a real horror". 2. I expect I wasn't in ..... very good condition that night. 3. The patient is still in ..... critical condition. 4. All agreed that the body was in ..... healthy condition. 5. The doctor said that he had had ..... considerable experience in midwifery. 6. Suddenly they both were in ..... immensely good humour. 7. He was relaxed now and in ..... better humour. 8. You are not in ..... very good mood this morning. 9. We're in ..... much better shape now than when we came here. 10. The machines that arrived yesterday weren't in ..... much better shape. 11. He is in ..... much better state now.

253 Fill in *a(n)* where necessary.

1. I have an uncle who is ..... architect. 2. He is ..... member of the city council. 3. As ..... conductor he was a great success, but as ..... composer he failed pitifully. 4. He came dressed as ..... pirate. 5. When Sawley's duties as ..... waiter were over, he changed into his blue jacket and came back to his cubby hole in the hall. 6. He served the nation as ..... commander in three wars. 7. He served as ..... mayor for several years. 8. The sleeping bag served as ..... bed. 9. Your title will be ..... Assistant Director of Special Projects, and you will be responsible directly to me. 10. His appointment as ..... instructor came as a surprise to everyone. 11. Wellesley College offered her a job as ..... instructress in mathematics, and she excelled at it all the time she was there. 12. He is ..... Professor of Pathology at Aberdeen University. 13. He is ..... lecturer in forensic medicine at Aberdeen University. 14. He accepted the post of ..... headmaster. 15. He wore the uniform of the British Army and held the rank of ..... Major. 16. A disused fire station served for ..... clubhouse.

254 Fill in *a(n)* where necessary.

1. I am your friend, but in my capacity as ..... officer of the law I must take you into custody. 2. I am here in my capacity as ..... chairman of the board. 3. Dr Smith was present, but in the quality of ..... friend, not as ..... physician. 4. They want to give her a Venetian vase as ..... farewell present. 5. A policeman had to act as ..... interpreter for her.

The Indefinite Article

255 Fill in *a(n)* where necessary.

1. I've got ..... splitting headache. 2. I've got ..... terrible toothache. 3. Certain problems are beginning to trouble me like ..... toothache. 4. Jim does very poorly in this foul New York winter, he always has ..... earache or .... sore throat. 5. He was suffering from ..... violent stomach ache.

256 Fill in *a(n)* where necessary.

1. After ..... two days' march the three of them jumped a goods train near Sandsbridge which took them to a place called Redfield. 2. The school was ..... three minutes' walk away. 3. We now had only about ..... twenty minutes' walk ahead of us. 4. The cottage is ..... few minutes' walk away. 5. What you're telling us is ..... old hat. 6. Then they drank ..... health to George VI and Richard I. 7. When I was around him, I was subconsciously compelled to speak ..... almost perfect English. 8. The hall porter looked round Miss Brown's room for any signs of ..... cat. 9. What ..... brand of ..... cigarette do you prefer? 10. What ..... kind of ..... suit was he wearing? 11. He is vain to ..... high degree. 12. Our safety depends in ..... great measure on how well we can all learn to do our jobs. 13. To ..... great extent he is himself to blame for his misfortune. 14. I agree with him to ..... certain extent. 15. That is the sort of ..... thing I had in mind.

257 Sentences for translation.

1. Er schreibt nun schon seit vier Stunden ohne Unterbrechung. 2. Warum fahren wir zur Abwechslung nicht mal nach Mallorca? 3. Ich bin schrecklich in Eile. 4. Sie nimmt großen Anteil an allem, was er tut. 5. Wir sind in der Lage, Ihnen die gewünschten Waren zu liefern. 6. In der Regel arbeitet er abends nicht. 7. Er hat es sich zur Regel gemacht, seinen Untergebenen gegenüber Distanz zu wahren. 8. Ich habe noch eine Arbeit zu erledigen. 9. Wollen wir einen Kaffee trinken? 10. Sie kocht einen ausgezeichneten Kaffee. 11. In der Gegend bekommt man einen ausgezeichneten Wein. 12. Ein Caruso ist er nicht gerade. 13. Wir verdanken ihr eine äußerst wichtige Information. 14. Sie können immer zu mir kommen, wenn Sie einen Rat brauchen. 15. Das war eine Hitze! 16. Das war ein Spaß! 17. Ich hatte vielleicht eine Angst! 18. Wir hatten einen Hunger! 19. Hast du eine Ahnung! 20. Was für ein Auto hast du? 21. Was für ein Mann ist er? 22. Was für eine Art von Anzug trug der Verdächtige? 23. In was für einer Branche sind Sie? 24. Diese Vogelart ist hier äußerst selten. 25. Er starb als Millionär. 26. Man könnte ihn als Fahrer ausbilden lassen. 27. Du kannst die Schachtel als Andenken behalten. 28. Diese Schrauben kosten zehn new pence das Dutzend. 29. Geben Sie mir bitte noch ein Glas Whisky! 30. Als Engländer muß man die Bibel lesen. 31. Mach doch nicht solchen Lärm! 32. Ich habe eine gute Nachricht für dich. 33. Hat das Kind Fieber? 34. Es tut mir leid, aber ich bin nicht in der Lage, Ihnen zu helfen.

-self Pronouns

258 -*self* pronouns. – Sentences for observation.

1. a) For a moment he could not *nerve himself* to open the parcel.
   b) He *oriented himself* quickly.
   c) In the next half-hour Joyce *washed* and *dressed* and cooked and wiped and toasted and poured and admonished and was lost.
   d) He *bathed*, *dressed*, and went upstairs.
   e) He sagged into a sitting position and *undressed himself*.
   f) When opportunity *offered*, he went to a barber's in one of the little streets behind Bond Street and had a haircut.
   g) We *cooked ourselves* some dinner and ate it.
   h) He'll *drink himself* to death if he goes on like that.
2. a) He is not the sort of man to raise a hand *against himself*.
   b) She stared *at herself* in the mirror.
   c) The guard could not see six feet *beyond himself*.
   d) He got a blanket and pulled it *over himself*.
   e) She looked *about her* in a dazed way.
   f) Charles stared *about him*, almost *beside himself*.
   g) The fog's awful; you can't see a yard *ahead of you*.
   h) He smiled *to himself*.
   i) You have to be true *to yourself*.
   j) *Between ourselves* I have no doubt that he is mistaken in this case.
3. a) He was remembering that this was the diagnosis on which Pearson and *himself* had differed.
   b) He had arranged to take Paddy and *myself* to a lodging house south of the river.
   c) John *himself* told me.
   d) I drank it *myself*.

259 Sentences for translation.

1. Leutnant Tomaselli hatte sich als fähiger Verwaltungsmann erwiesen. 2. Junge Leute sonnten sich auf den Bänken im Park. 3. Sie schminkt sich immer ein bißchen zu stark. 4. Meine beiden Brüder und ich hatten früher eine Fabrik. 5. Mein einziger Bruder ist Musiker wie ich. 6. Joan badete, parfümierte sich, schminkte sich sorgfältig und zog einen enganliegenden grün-goldenen Hausanzug aus chinesischer Seide an. 7. Sheila blickte mit unverhohlener Ehrfurcht um sich. 8. Er schlug die Tür hinter sich zu. 9. Die alte Dame wohnte ganz für sich. 10. Hör auf! Du willst dich doch nicht lächerlich machen. 11. Aber behalte das bitte für dich. 12. Er stand auf, verbeugte sich, als sie einander vorgestellt wurden, und fiel beinahe über das Tischchen, das vor ihm stand. 13. Du hast dein ganzes Leben noch vor dir. 14. Ihre Augen füllten sich mit Tränen. 15. Die junge Dame hat sich zu ihrem Vorteil verändert. 16. Die Milch wird sich bei diesem Wetter nicht lange halten. 17. Ich fühle mich heute hundeelend.

18. Mutter erholte sich nur langsam von ihrer schweren Krankheit. 19. Er weigerte sich, mir diesen kleinen Gefallen zu erweisen. 20. Langsam öffnete sich die Tür. 21. Man kann nur hoffen, daß sich so etwas nie wieder ereignet. 22. Du solltest dich wirklich schämen. 23. Wenn ich nur wüßte, wo dieser Feigling sich versteckt hält. 24. Je älter er wird, desto schlechter benimmt er sich. 25. Sie können es sich ruhig bequem machen.

Possessive Adjectives

260 Possessive adjectives. – Sentences for observation.

1. She jumped to *her* feet and felt the handle of the glue brush.
2. They grabbed her by *the* feet.
3. What have you got in *your* mouth?
4. She kissed him on *the* mouth.
5. He was holding a dead sparrow in *his* hand.
6. The woman shook him warmly by *the* hand.
7. I'm sure he's got something up *his* sleeve.
8. He took Eaves by *the* sleeve.
9. She felt very weak at *the* knees.
10. Heavy bulges rose over *his* brows, to intersect the vertical creases on *the* forehead.
11. She was in *her* late thirties, and looked it.
12. A man in *the* late forties with a dark red face and thick lips came by degrees into the room.
13. Place the victim in a face-up position, put something under *his* shoulders to raise them, and allow *his* head to drop backward; kneel above the victim's head and grasp *his* arms at *the* wrists, crossing and pressing *his* wrists against *his* lower chest; pull *the* arms upward, outward, and backward as far as possible and repeat 15 times per minute. If another person is present, he should tilt the victim's head backward so that *his* jaw juts forward.
14. If the injured person is in no imminent danger, it is far safer to leave him lying where he is. A rolled-up jersey or coat placed under *the* head, and a coat or blanket over him is the best treatment you can give while waiting for help. If the person is unconscious, loosen *the* clothing, especially round *the* neck.

261 Choose what you consider to be the more suitable of the words in brackets.

1. He shrugged (the, his) shoulders. 2. He was a bulky man in (the, his) seventies. 3. She had gone down to make herself a cup of coffee, but had tripped at the top of the stairs and fallen to (the, her) death. 4. He kissed her on (the, her) forehead. 5. He stared me straight in (the, my) eye. 6. I couldn't look her in (the, her) eyes. 7. They looked each other full in (the, their) face. 8. She began to snivel dangerously, and he quickly patted her on (the, her) hand. 9. He pecked Betty on (the, her) cheek and shook Richard heartily by (the, his) hand. 10. He took me by (the, my) arm. 11. The old man shook (the, his) head. 12. That boy has always got (the, his) hands in (the, his) pockets. 13. They were all sitting round the open fire: Father had (the, his) pipe in (the, his) mouth, Mother had (the, her) knitting in (the, her) lap, and the dog had a bone between (the, its) teeth.

Interrogatives. – Sentences for observation.

262

1. *Who* do you imagine would have asked me out to lunch?
2. *Who* do you love?
3. *Who* did you kill?
4. *Who* do I see about getting a discharge?
5. *Who* do you suppose they were really trying to kill?
6. *Who* Britain Wants for President. (Newspaper headline)
7. I don't care a damn *who* I work *for*.
8. I walked up to the information desk in the lobby of the New York Times building, and said to a tired-looking woman there, "*Whom* do I see to apply for a job?" I emphasized the "whom" to show her that I had mastered grammar.
9. *What's* today? – June the twenty-sixth, 1970.
10. *What* are the cornflakes *like*?
11. Always have a neat collar, then you'll look presentable, no matter *how* your suit looks.
12. Being of such good repute, *how comes* it that you are prepared to use a document which is obtained in such deplorable circumstances?
13. Long time no see. *How's* tricks?
14. And *in what* does that young man instruct the younger generation?
15. *What* was Vernon talking to you *about*?
16. *What's* the party in aid *of*?
17. *With what* plans had they come?
18. *What* part of Ireland do you come *from*?
19. *What* time does he get home?

Sentences for translation.

263

1. Wen kennst du in New York? 2. Wen wolltest du denn treffen? 3. Wen wird man außer mir schon verdächtigen? 4. Was glaubst du denn, mit wem du redest? 5. Für wen arbeiten Sie? 6. An wen denkst du denn? 7. Ich weiß nicht mehr, wem ich sie gegeben habe. 8. Was gibt's zu Mittag? 9. Schaun wir doch mal, was es im Fernsehen gibt! 10. Wie ist das Wetter? 11. Wozu hast du es denn weggenommen? 12. Woran glaubst du? 13. Worauf führen Sie seinen Tod zurück? 14. Welchem Umstand verdanke ich die Ehre Ihres Besuches? 15. Was für eine Haarfarbe hat er? 16. Wie groß sind Sie? 17. Aus welchem Teil von Schottland kommen Sie? 18. Um welche Zeit bist du gestern nach Hause gekommen? 19. Wie gefallen Ihnen die schottischen Seen? 20. Woher kommst du gerade? 21. Wofür tust du das? 22. Welches von diesen beiden Büchern gehört ihr? 23. Welchen von diesen beiden Hüten ziehst du vor? 24. Ich weiß nicht, worüber du sprichst. 25. „Ich denke angestrengt nach." – „Worüber?" 26. „Er wird sich umbringen." – „Warum denn?" 27. „Sprich mit ihm!" – „Worüber denn?" 28. „Schreib einen Brief!" – „Wem denn?" 29. „Schreib einen Brief an Rumble Bagwasher!" – „An wen?" 30. „Er heiratete sie wegen ihres Geldes." – „Weswegen?" 31. „Misch das Getränk mit Apfelsaft!" – „Womit?"

Relative Clauses

264 Supply relative pronouns and punctuation where necessary.

1. The British pound ..... has been ailing for decades has begun to show signs of returning health. 2. The inquest on Mrs Hood ..... opened on September 27 produced little ..... might help to detect her murderer and no further clues to her real identity. 3. Half a grain of morphia is a very substantial dose ..... effects might easily persist for several days. 4. They were all assembled outside the house ..... low roof was deep in autumn leaves. 5. She occupied a ground-floor bedroom ..... window descended into the area some eighteen inches below the level of the street. 6. I had thought there would be time to read all the books ..... titles I had jotted down. 7. Lewis relaxed in the enormous armchair ..... springs had been broken to his weight. 8. I stepped into a large room ..... ample windows opened upon St Ann's Square. 9. He never used torture on prisoners ..... he knew would not break under torture. 10. Many thanks for the interesting talk with Professor Stevenson ..... I much enjoyed meeting. 11. It was Betty ..... I was at the concert with. 12. Gordon was sent to wretched, pretentious schools ..... fees were round about a hundred and twenty pounds a year. 13. They were the kind of people ..... in every conceivable activity, even if it is only getting on to a bus, are automatically elbowed away from the heart of things. 14. Of course it was money ..... was at the bottom of it, always money. 15. Gordon walked homeward against the rattling wind ..... blew his hair backward and gave him more of a "good" forehead than ever. 16. James ..... came home for his midday dinner paid twenty-seven and six a week. 17. He was one of the shop's best customers – a flitting, solitary creature ..... was almost too shy to speak and ..... by some strange manipulation kept himself always a day away from a shave. 18. The sense of disintegration, of decay ..... is endemic in our time, was strong upon him. 19. The companies countered with an offer ..... they boasted was their "biggest and best ever" – and the unions snubbed it as "completely unacceptable".

265 Sentences for translation.

1. Du bist derjenige, der handeln muß. 2. Du bist der Feigling, nicht ich! 3. Sie waren es, die uns mit Nachrichten versorgten. 4. Ich bin es, der sich langweilt! 5. Er setzte sich in einen Sessel, dessen Kissen aus einem Bündel alter Zeitungen bestand, die mit einem Bindfaden zusammengebunden waren. 6. Ich bin nicht aus dem Holz, aus dem Helden geschnitzt sind. 7. Das ist etwas, worauf du stolz sein solltest. 8. In großen Höhen liegt tiefer Schnee, der zum Teil bis in den Sommer liegenbleibt. 9. Er zeugte zwölf Kinder, von denen elf überlebten. 10. Im oberen Zimmer döste Mr Busby, der selten ins Geschäft herunterkam, über einer in Kalbsleder gebundenen Ausgabe von Middletons *Travels in the Levant*. 11. So, das ist also Margaret, von der ich ja schon soviel gehört habe! 12. In der Zimmerdecke war ein Riß, der der Karte Australiens glich. 13. Niemand verdient es mehr als du, Charlie. 14. Es gibt keinen Mann in meiner Abteilung, der

Relative Clauses

nicht von Keith Mallory gehört hat. 15. Es gab kaum eine Familie, die nicht irgendeinen Grund gehabt hätte, die Polizei zu fürchten. 16. Was Mary an schwerem Gepäck besaß, war bereits vom Zoll abgefertigt. 17. Die Zeit, die ihm noch verblieb, widmete er seiner Frau und seinen Kindern.

Sentences for translation.

266

1. Sie ging schon ins Haus, während er noch nach einer Stelle suchte, wo er den Wagen parken konnte. 2. Wir fanden eine Stelle, wo man schön im Freien essen konnte. 3. Der Strand war verlassen, und es war niemand da, der sie hätte hören können. 4. Hier ist ein Herr, der Sie sprechen möchte. 5. Ich werde dir einige Bücher über Hypnose bringen, die du lesen kannst. 6. Ich möchte ein Zimmer, in dem ich schlafen kann. 7. Es war ein Anblick, der jedes Vaterherz erfreut hätte. 8. Seine Schwiegermutter ist ohne Zweifel ein Faktor, mit dem man rechnen muß. 9. Ihm fiel nichts ein, was er hätte sagen können. 10. Der alte Mann brauchte ganz offensichtlich jemand, der sich um ihn kümmerte. 11. Ich bin einsam und brauche jemand, mit dem ich mich unterhalten kann. 12. Er war kein Mann, der den gleichen Fehler zweimal machte. 13. Sie ist keine Frau, die man warten läßt. 14. Er war kein Mensch, der schnell Freundschaften schloß. 15. Er ist nicht der Typ, der eine einmal gefaßte Meinung ändert. 16. Ich bin es, der hier Befehle gibt! 17. Der Kapitän war der letzte, der das Schiff verließ. 18. Der Hausmeister ist der letzte, der die alte Dame noch lebend gesehen hat. 19. Sie ist die einzige, die ihn ungestraft Piggy nennen darf. 20. Sie war die einzige, die es bemerkte. 21. Er war der einzige Gast im Hotel, der zu dieser Stunde noch auf war. 22. Er war entschlossen, den ersten Mann, der vorbeikam, zu überfallen. 23. Dies waren die ersten Worte, die er seit seiner Ankunft gesprochen hatte. 24. Er war der einzige Herrscher, der mit seinen Truppen an die Front ging. 25. Er war einer der wenigen, denen Skeffington aufmerksam zuhörte.

Case Problems

267 Case problems. – Sentences for observation.

1. For the second time he had behaved very badly and yet had made her feel as if it were *she* who was in the wrong.
2. "I'm afraid it's *I* who want you back for a moment," said the judge.
3. Doubtless it was *they* who were singing.
4. It's not *I*, it's *you* who don't understand!
5. When the telephone rang, he imagined it might be *she*.
6. Are you sure it is *she*?
7. The only thing that interests him is *him*.
8. Is that *him*?
9. Bob and Peter came in. He knew it was *them*.
10. Meanwhile Julia, who was five years older than *he*, received as good as no education at all.
11. She is older than *I*.
12. Though he was probably a few years younger than *me*, he was nearly bald.
13. There can be absolutely no question of *my* hating him.
14. There can be absolutely no question of *me* hating him.
15. It's no good *your* writing to the flat because I moved out this morning.
16. Her spectacles caught the light and prevented *him* seeing where she was looking.
17. Even in criminal cases I have known police officers obtain evidence unlawfully, but that doesn't prevent *it* being used as evidence.
18. I suppose you thought it funny, *me* suddenly coming in like that?
19. He gave us the money for you and *I* to share.
20. Nothing was learned of the robbers' plans and little of *they* themselves.

Some & any

Some and *any*. – Sentences for observation.

268

1. a) Didn't he have *some* trouble in Holland?
   b) Aren't there *some* you won't need?
   c) Doesn't she have *some* rooms to rent?
   d) Can't *something* more be done?
   e) Why don't you say *something*?
   f) Isn't there *something* else you can do besides read the damn newspapers all day?
2. a) Would you like *some* whisky – or brandy?
   b) Would you like *something* to eat before you leave?
   c) Would you like *something*? Refreshment of *some* kind?
   d) Will you have *some* soup?
   e) Can we have *some* milk?
3. a) Why should we put *some* more money into that old car?
   b) Mike, is *something* wrong?
   c) Has it *something* to do with your religion?
   d) Did I say *something* funny?
   e) Is *something* wrong, Deborah? Is there *something* you want to ask?
   f) The receptionist looked at him with dislike. "Did you want *something*?" – "A room." – "A what?"
   g) Had I been watched? Had *someone* followed me?
   h) Is it *someone* who was on the boat?
   i) Why should he have let *someone* in on the job, when there were a dozen ways in which he could have carried it out himself?
   j) Are you looking for *something*?
4. a) Knowledge is not *something* that can be bought.
   b) Even when he wasn't doing *something* tiresome, like winding up the bucket, had it really been satisfactory?
   c) It was a period of activity akin to that of the War years, but without *some* of the restraint of those years.
   d) It was not possible for him to bring *some* fish back to pay for the cost of the fuel he used.
   e) This Coronation business is not giving much of a chance to *some* of our former favourites in the news columns.
   f) I don't want *some* of the money, I want all of it.
   g) *Somebody* did not hand in his homework.
5. a) If you have *any* difficulty, let me know.
   b) If you've had *some* experience, you won't find the work hard.
   c) If you can produce *something* to show that the local authority is dealing with the matter, that might help you.
   d) "I hate him for being so disgustingly pi," he would have said if *somebody* had asked him to explain his hatred.
   e) I could do with a little more if there is still *some* left.

Some & any

    f) If *someone* were to offer me money for the letter, I would accept it gratefully.

6. a) I was passing by and I felt I ought to drop in and offer you *any* assistance you might need, since you apparently have only limited time here.
   b) The clerk can tell him *anything* he wants to know.
   c) You can ask *any* man you meet.

269 Fill in *some* or *any* in the following sentences. In cases where *some* as well as *any* may be used, explain the difference in meaning.

1. Won't you have ..... tea? 2. Didn't you buy ..... cigars this morning? 3. I know you bought ..... cigars. 4. Will you take ..... fruit? 5. Why are ..... of the houses in this area still without electricity? 6. Are ..... of the houses in this area still without electricity? 7. ..... student has been trying to reach you. 8. Surely there's ..... way of stopping him. 9. ..... of the neighbours would be glad to help. 10. There isn't ..... flour in the house. 11. If we had ..... time left, we'd go on to Brighton. 12. I'll come to your house ..... day next week. 13. ..... friend of Father's has his car today. 14. If we have ..... visitors, we'll make lemonade. 15. Tom has hardly ..... close friends. 16. ..... visitors came by while you were out. 17. ..... good doctor could have told him what was wrong with him. 18. We stayed there for ..... years. 19. I could certainly eat ..... more chicken. 20. If there's ..... coffee, I'll have ..... 21. He speaks better English than ..... other student in the class. 22. Doesn't she have ..... rooms to rent? 23. She did the work without ..... help. 24. ..... students who want to leave now may do so. 25. Don't you need ..... more money? 26. Are there ..... other questions that you'd like to ask? 27. He didn't answer ..... of my questions, he answered all of them. 28. Consult ..... expert you like, they'll all tell you the same. 29. He managed to stay there for ten days without spending ..... money. 30. Isn't there ..... whisky left in the bottle? 31. I don't know ..... man who would be more suitable.

It & es

270 *It.* – Sentences for observation and translation.

1. *It* was a bit of luck my meeting you this morning.
2. But *it* is never by accident that I find myself looking through that open door.
3. *It* so happened that both were very good workmen.
4. *It* was when he was seventeen that his father died, leaving about two hundred pounds.
5. He stood firm when *it* came to the country's vital interests.
6. He was a good tennis player and looked *it*.

271 Equivalents of German *es.* – Sentences for translation.

1. Das Volk hungert, es ist mutlos und erschöpft. 2. Es sind noch vierzehn Tage bis Weihnachten. 3. Es ist niemand hier. 4. Es geht nichts über eine heiße Tasse Tee mit Rum und einen brennenden Kamin. 5. Es hat sich vieles geändert. 6. Es wird einmal die Zeit kommen, wo du für jedes Stückchen Brot dankbar bist. 7. Es gefällt mir hier sehr gut. 8. Es ist mir klar, daß es nicht immer so glatt gehen kann. 9. Wenn er es für richtig hält, das überall auszuposaunen, dann soll er nur. 10. Es täte mir leid, wenn du meintest, ich schätze deinen Rat nicht. 11. Ohne Geld geht es nun mal nicht. 12. Es wurde ein glanzvoller Abend. 13. Es wird nicht mehr lange dauern, bis die Bahn kommt. 14. Es wird vermutet, daß sie sich in Chicago getroffen haben. 15. Bist du es, Jonathan? 16. Wer war es? – Es waren die Kinder. 17. Was gibt's zum Frühstück? 18. Was gibt's im Fernsehen? 19. In diesem Hause spukt's. 20. Es hat geklopft. 21. Es wurde gesungen, getanzt und viel gelacht. 22. Es heißt, er sei sehr reich. 23. In London lebt es sich gut. 24. Du weißt, er meint es gut mit dir. 25. Wir haben es noch nie so gut gehabt. 26. Wir brauchen jemand, der Kohlen holt. – Was kriege ich, wenn ich es mache? 27. Soll ich die Maschine abstellen? – Ja, bitte tun Sie es. 28. Es bestand kein Grund, den Beruf zu wechseln, und trotzdem haben es viele getan. 29. Ist die Hütte eingeschneit? – Ich befürchte es. 30. Er wird gute Arbeit leisten. – Ich hoffe es. 31. Wird die Show ausverkauft sein? – Ich hoffe es nicht. 32. Werden wir rechtzeitig in Leeds sein? – Ich glaube es nicht. 33. Wird er sich damit zufriedengeben? – Ich glaube es nicht. 34. Wird er bis zum Abend zurück sein? – Ich weiß es nicht. 35. Meine Frau ist entsetzt, und ich bin es auch. 36. Er ist langsam und pedantisch und wird es auch immer bleiben. 37. Er war sehr schüchtern und blieb es sein Leben lang.

Comparison

272 Supply the comparative or superlative form of the words in brackets.

1. This is just about the (awkward) thing that ever happened to me. 2. He was growing (bitter) and (bitter). 3. Laver hit every type of shot with such power, precision, and authority, that Cox was under the (cruel) pressure from the start. 4. I was surprised at the tempestuousness of her passion, but the more it rose, the (dead) I felt inside. 5. He gave her his (friendly) smile. 6. He looked (gaunt) than I have ever seen him. 7. I have never seen people (glum) at their pleasures. 8. The boy is getting (handsome) all the time. 9. Almost two hundred of the city's (handsome) bronze statues were torn down. 10. How was I to know she was (ill) than she looked? 11. The next flight of stairs was even (narrow). 12. He thought he had never spent a (pleasant) evening in his life. 13. It was probably the (pleasant) and (thrilling) moment of her life. 14. I haven't the (remote) idea of what could bring a detective inspector out from Carlisle to see me. 15. Friends (sober) than he had rushed him to the airport. 16. A newspaper dies hard, lingering on until even the (stubborn) owners realize that the only answer is a mercy killing. 17. You're far (stupid) than I thought. 18. It's the (stupid) idea I ever heard of! 19. He looked (tired) than she had ever seen him. 20. She looked even (tired), and her coat was wet. 21. He was undoubtedly the (calm) and (collected) of the four, or at least seemed so. 22. The half-darkness was helping me to sound (calm) than I was feeling. 23. The general feeling in the town was neither (serene) nor (calm). 24. She seemed freer, (mature), more of a woman. 25. She had moved into middle age getting almost (beautiful) as she went on, becoming (thin) and (elegant), and her hair still black as anything.

273 Choose what you consider to be the correct form, pointing out cases where either alternative would be correct.

1. They received no (fewer, less) than 1,400 letters in response to their appeal. 2. The (fewest, least) suicides take place in December, the most in April and May. 3. The building has (fewer, less) floor space than the Empire State, yet it contains no (fewer, less) than 1,200 offices. 4. Not many of these buildings are (fewer, less) than thirty years old. 5. Sometimes I wish you had (fewer, less) brains and more heart. 6. She makes (fewer, less) demands on his time than you do. 7. In England, justice is handed out swiftly and surely, and as a result there are (fewer, less) murders in the entire kingdom of Great Britain yearly than there are in the City of Chicago. 8. Then the road turns another bend, past a wood – and a hundred yards (farther, further) stands Jeremy's cottage, also thatched, and with a small, neat garden. 9. The (nearest, next) morning I shoved the letter into the (nearest, next) mailbox. 10. His (eldest, oldest) son got drafted.

274 Comment on the following sentences.

1. They were more stunned than amused.
2. That Bentley was more shrewd than scrupulous can hardly be doubted.
3. It was more strange than terrible.

Sentences for translation.

1. Es waren nicht weniger als 45 goldene Uhren im Koffer des Schmugglers. 2. Du bist auch nicht kränker als ich. 3. Je eher es vorbei ist, desto besser! 4. Er wurde immer erfolgreicher und immer reicher. 5. Das Spiel wurde immer schneller und immer spannender. 6. Ich weiß das so gut wie du. 7. Das Fahrrad ist so gut wie neu. 8. Er bezähmte seine Ungeduld so gut er konnte. 9. Er säuberte seinen Anzug so gut er konnte. 10. Am weitaus schwersten betroffen ist England, das normalerweise zwei Drittel seines Öls aus arabischen Quellen bezieht. 11. Wir müssen ihn so bald wie möglich ins nächste Krankenhaus schaffen. 12. Er schlich sich aus dem Haus und ging hinunter zur nächsten Bushaltestelle. 13. Es ist höchst seltsam. 14. Er ist am gefährlichsten, wenn er still ist. 15. Wir wollen doch mal sehen, wer am schnellsten rudern kann. 16. Wenn es zum Schlimmsten kommt, werden wir telegraphieren.

Adjectives in Noun Function

276 Supply the prop word *one* or a suitable noun where necessary.

1. There were also some sick ..... there. 2. In spite of the electricity shortage, one of the lifts was maintained to carry the ill ..... and the feeble ..... back and forth between their rooms and the dining hall. 3. There are wounded ..... everywhere and we can hear the guns like thunder all round us. 4. The 141-page report showed for the first time just how bad things really are for Britain's coloured ..... 5. Some sick ..... are very dependent upon the emotional support of others. 6. It is not unusual for a very sick ..... to feel more upset about another person in the ward than he is about himself. 7. I daresay the black ..... in Uganda or the Fijians or the Indians might be less choosy. 8. The point is that the rich ..... play an essential role in modern society. 9. Inevitably the process was slow, and many sick ..... and injured ..... died before they could be properly attended to. 10. Farmers are always the first ..... to desert in a battle. They are also the first ..... to be collaborators. 11. His left leg was shorter than his right ..... 12. His sermons were the same ..... he had given in Connecticut and Long Island. 13. She was not the only ..... of the family to become famous. 14. Leamas was not a reflective man and not a particularly philosophical ..... either. 15. As to shoes, he would like brown ....., with triangular brass eyeholes according to the latest fashion. 16. The trouble is there are no rich supporters left. Only poor ..... 17. He had a good reason for not wanting police-court publicity, but Charles had a better ..... 18. The first callers arrive for breakfast and the last ..... leave long after midnight. 19. "How much are the grapes?" the man asked, and was told that the black ..... were sixpence, the green ..... fourpence a pound. "Well then, give us half a pound of the black .....," the man ordered. 20. The crime for which a poisoner is arrested is usually not his first ....., nor even his second ..... 21. He had bought her a scarf of the kind she wanted, but a green ..... instead of a pink ..... 22. It is my opinion that a child following natural instincts prefers to use his left hand rather than his right ..... 23. Do you think that English girls are nicer than American ..... ?

277 Sentences for translation.

1. Die Griechen begruben ihre Toten während der Nacht und ließen die Verwundeten auf dem Schlachtfeld liegen. 2. Alle Anwesenden zerschmolzen in Tränen. 3. Unter den Anwesenden befanden sich auch der englische Botschafter und seine Gattin. 4. Dies ist ein sehr zartes Grün. Ich habe vier verschiedene Arten von Grün in meinem Farbkasten. 5. Der Beleidigte hat den ersten Schuß, nicht wahr, Herr Oberst? 6. Der Angeklagte schien sich über die Vorgänge im Gerichtssaal zu amüsieren. 7. Aus dem Obigen wollen Sie bitte ersehen, welchen Posten ich augenblicklich innehabe. 8. Das folgende entnehmen wir dem Christian Science Monitor. 9. Dabei kommt bestimmt nichts Gutes heraus. 10. Das Unmögliche erledigen wir sofort, Wunder dauern etwas länger. 11. Sie verlangen Unmög-

Adjectives in Noun Function

liches. 12. Ich erzählte ihr nur das Wichtigste. 13. Das Dringlichste muß erledigt werden, ehe wir etwas anderes in Angriff nehmen. 14. Dieser Artikel enthält viel Interessantes. 15. Ich hasse alles Gemeine. 16. Die Gegend bot in dieser Jahreszeit nichts Anziehendes. 17. Das ist wirklich das Allerneueste. 18. Von den lebenden Komponisten ist er zweifellos der beliebteste. 19. Meine Tante hat eine braune Katze und zwei schwarze. 20. Ich mag diesen Tee nicht. Haben Sie keinen besseren? 21. Kranken wird oft schon geholfen, wenn jemand einfach ihren Klagen Beachtung schenkt. 22. Das ist unser bestes Zimmer. Wir vermieten es oft an Neuvermählte. 23. Die Männer in diesem Werk wollen nicht mit Farbigen zusammenarbeiten.

Adverbs

278 Adjective or adverb? – Put in the correct form.

1. He was certainly born (lucky). 2. (Lucky), the baby was not born on the thirteenth. 3. We tied up the dog (loose), so that it could move (easy). 4. The shutter broke (loose). 5. That cake came out (splendid). 6. The pudding came out too (sweet). 7. Her hair was cut (short). 8. He was so thirsty that he could have drunk his water bottle (dry). 9. He felt (bad) from eating green apples. 10. The brandy had made him feel (good). 11. The blind man felt his way about (cautious). 12. He felt (quick) in his pockets for the money. 13. Why can't the boy keep his nose (clean)? 14. He tried to interfere, and was knocked (unconscious). 15. I must have pressed the button (unconscious). 16. Sally looked (beautiful) with her hair fluttering in the wind. 17. His secretary looked (careful) through the papers. 18. He looked at me (furious). 19. I saw our neighbour striding off looking (furious). 20. The teacher looked (weary) as he walked home after school. 21. The teacher looked (weary) at the pile of work on his desk. 22. The policeman looked at the man (suspicious). 23. The man looked (suspicious) to the policeman. 24. She painted the cupboard (white). 25. She painted the cupboard (careful). 26. Continually surrounded with every sort of trouble and never thinking of himself, he nonetheless passed his whole life (healthy), (happy) and (rich). 27. A man is presumed (innocent) until he is proved (guilty). 28. The coffee smells (good). 29. The man smelt (strong) of whisky. 30. "All right, do it the way you think (right)," she said, sounding (disappointed). 31. Charles stood (motionless), his face dead white. 32. This wine tastes rather (sour), doesn't it? 33. He tasted the soup (cautious). 34. This soup tastes (strong) of fish. 35. He smelt very (unpleasant). 36. Anyone who holds life so (cheap) is capable of hastening the death of an unwanted wife. 37. Here he lived very (cheap), writing books and some music.

279 Complete the following sentences.

Examples: An attentive listener listens . . . . .
An attentive listener listens attentively.
An early riser gets up . . . . .
An early riser gets up early.

1. An awkward dancer dances . . . . . 2. A brave soldier fights . . . . . 3. A careful driver drives . . . . . 4. A childish person behaves . . . . . 5. A daily newspaper appears . . . . . 6. A direct train goes there . . . . . 7. A fair person will always treat you . . . . . 8. A fluent speaker talks . . . . . 9. A good player plays . . . . . 10. A hard worker works . . . . . 11. An hourly train runs . . . . . 12. A latecomer arrives . . . . 13. A light sleeper sleeps . . . . . 14. A modest man acts . . . . . 15. A pretty girl looks . . . . . 16. A rough player plays . . . . . 17. A slow eater eats . . . . . 18. A soft-spoken person speaks . . . . . 19. A weekly magazine is published . . . . .

Adverb with or without -*ly*? – Put in the correct form. **280**

1. In the evening they were all (dead) tired. 2. That man is (disgusting) successful. 3. His English was almost (embarrassing) colloquial. 4. Although it was a (burning) hot day, the inside of the cellar was (icy) cold. 5. "It's (jolly) cold," he said with chattering teeth. 6. She had (precious) little time for her job. 7. Things look (pretty) bad for him. 8. I am (shocking) bad at languages. 9. He was (soaking) wet. 10. The place was (spotless) clean. 11. It was (stifling) hot. 12. The time passed (terrible) slowly. 13. When I came to his bed, the boy was (wide) awake. 14. The detective found the door (wide) open.

Adverb with or without -*ly*? – Put in the correct form. **281**

1. The sun was shining (bright). 2. The fire was burning (bright) and (clear). 3. Don't sell it too (cheap). 4. In Japan we lived astonishingly (cheap). 5. The prisoners were (close) guarded. 6. He was following (close) behind. 7. The victory was (dear) won. 8. Their excessive caution had cost them (dear). 9. He makes a large profit by buying (cheap) and selling (dear). 10. I've (clean) forgotten the name. 11. He was decently dressed and (clean)-shaven. 12. She was (deep) hurt by his remark. 13. They didn't have to dig (deep) to find water. 14. If you (hard) ever work, you can't expect to succeed. 15. If you work (hard), you will succeed. 16. Henderson aims (high) in his political ambitions. 17. Cholera is a disease (high) dreaded in the East. 18. He took the bad news (light). 19. Experienced campers travel (light). 20. She spoke (slow), (loud), and very (distinct). 21. Don't talk so (loud). 22. He stood up and bowed (low) before the old lady. 23. Don't value yourself too (low). 24. The policeman aimed (low), for the man's legs. 25. She was (pretty) dressed. 26. She was (pretty) tired. 27. You guessed (right). 28. She (right) guessed that he had written the letter himself. 29. When she returned, she found the children (sound) asleep. 30. He settled down on the hay and slept as (sound) as always. 31. The desk was (thick) covered with dust. 32. The frozen snow lay (thick) in the garden of the little villa. 33. The children sat with their hands (tight) clasped. 34. Shut the door (tight). 35. Everything is going (wrong) today. 36. My wife seldom guesses (wrong) on books. 37. There were a number of (wrong) spelt words in the text. 38. She was a (square)-built, energetic woman. 39. His teeth were (sparkling) clean. 40. In the window was a (new)-hung notice.

Sentences for translation. **282**

1. Sie hatte diese Arien herrlich gesungen. 2. Er hatte es völlig vergessen. 3. Wir bedauern das Versehen außerordentlich. 4. Er spricht ausgezeichnet Englisch. 5. Ich glaube fest an seine Unschuld. 6. Ich esse im allgemeinen in der Stadt zu Mittag. 7. Er rief laut um Hilfe. 8. Ich wollte ja nur diese Briefe einstecken.

Adverbs

9. Ich spiele immer noch gelegentlich Tennis. 10. Er arbeitet meistens zu Hause. 11. Ich weiß bereits die Lösung. 12. Ist der Briefträger schon dagewesen? 13. Er kommt immer abends. 14. Er hilft ihr immer beim Abwaschen. 15. Nie hilft er mir! 16. Ich treffe ihn oft am Bahnhof. 17. Er besucht oft seine Großeltern. 18. Wir gehen selten ins Kino. 19. Er will immer noch die Browns einladen. 20. Sie wartet immer noch auf dich.

283 Put in the correct form of the word in brackets.

1. He drained his glass (absent-minded). 2. He needed money (bad). 3. "I've had an accident," she said (breathless). 4. (Breathless), I watched him open the box. 5. They knocked on the door (sharp), and waited (breathless) for an answer. 6. He had always been able to beat the big man (effortless) at tennis. 7. So long as you play (fair) with me, everything is all right. 8. I'm sure this sweater fits (fine). 9. His shoes were (fresh) shined. 10. He talks (easy) and (good) and dresses in good taste. 11. The criminal is as (good) as caught. 12. He slept (long) and (heavy). 13. The thief was caught (red-handed). 14. He thought he could play it (safe). 15. He came back looking as if he had just conquered Everest (single-handed). 16. He sells all his paintings (private). 17. He went (quick) out of the office. 18. The waves broke (soundless) on the white sands of the beach. 19. She was scared (stiff). 20. "I don't quite see what you mean," he said (stiff). 21. On the stairs to the cellar he stopped (short). 22. It's (pretty) cold outside, but I'm dressed (warm). 23. I was a little afraid of the luncheon party, but everything went (swimming). 24. He was slumped (low) in his chair. 25. The girls laughed too (loud) and too (long). 26. She is a (high) strung person. 27. The mists hung (heavy) over London. 28. You know (full) well what I mean. 29. The body wasn't buried (deep) enough. 30. The blade was double-edged and awkward to hold. I cut my thumb (deep). 31. He was sleeping very (deep) that night. 32. She could see that he was (dead) serious. 33. On one count at least, Burbank had been (dead) right. 34. When you travel by Piper, you set your own schedule and fly (direct) to your destination. 35. Raising his voice he turned and looked (direct) at her. 36. I sensed that there was someone (direct) behind me.

284 Sentences for translation.

1. Langsam näherte sich der Einbrecher der Mauer. 2. Ein paar Meter entfernt blieb er plötzlich stehen. 3. Er lauschte aufmerksam. 4. Auf der anderen Seite der Mauer unterhielten sich laut zwei Männer. 5. Unser Einbrecher stand absolut regungslos. 6. Wie langsam doch die Zeit verging! 7. Schließlich wurden die Stimmen auf der anderen Seite schwächer. 8. Nach einer Weile war es vollkommen still. 9. Offensichtlich waren die beiden Männer weggegangen. 10. Leise ging der Einbrecher zum Eingangstor. 11. Nachdem er sich noch einmal verstohlen umgesehen hatte, nahm er schnell seine Werkzeuge heraus und begann,

an dem Schloß zu arbeiten. 12. Eine Viertelstunde lang arbeitete er angestrengt, und dann war das Tor endlich offen. 13. Nach weiteren zwanzig Minuten stand er vor dem Panzerschrank im Lohnbüro. 14. Er konnte kaum etwas sehen, und er traute sich nicht, seine Taschenlampe anzumachen. 15. Da er sich sehr müde fühlte, beschloß er, sich ein paar Minuten auszuruhen. 16. Gähnend sank er in einen Sessel und war im Nu fest eingeschlafen.

Sentences for translation. **285**

1. Sie schaute ihn bewundernd an. 2. Wir können Maschinen nicht so billig herstellen wie die Japaner. 3. Das Baby wurde tot geboren. 4. Er arbeitete bis tief in die Nacht. 5. Das ist leichter gesagt als getan. 6. Er geht fast nie zu Fuß. 7. Die Firma wurde von der Krise kaum betroffen. 8. Die Firma wurde von der Krise schwer betroffen. 9. Er zog einen frisch gebügelten Anzug an. 10. Er kam um Punkt neun Uhr an. 11. Warum schneidest du das Brot nicht etwas dicker? 12. Ich war bereits um sechs Uhr hellwach.

Put the adverbs in the most likely position. **286**

1. I thanked him. (breathlessly) 2. Think before you answer these questions. (carefully) 3. It is easier to point the path of wisdom out to others than to tread it oneself. (determinedly) 4. He laughed. (embarrassedly) 5. He coughed several times. (loudly) 6. We heard the sound of a bell. (suddenly) 7. All these books can be ordered from the publisher. (direct) 8. Jennifer looked into his eyes. (directly) 9. The door opened and Anne came in. (quietly) 10. He began to look about the room. (slowly) 11. He settled into a chair. (wearily) 12. She was still engaged in cleaning up. (busily) 13. The British police stand high in world esteem. (deservedly) 14. In later years she could have taken things more easily. (justifiably). 15. The onlookers began to realize that the sides were evenly matched. (slowly)

Decide in which of the following sentences *very* is used wrongly, and put them right. **287**

1. His speech has been very criticized by the press. 2. He was very agitated. 3. She seemed very amused. 4. His face seemed very changed in aspect. 5. I am very concerned about his health. 6. He is very disgusted with his domestic life. 7. They were very disturbed. 8. The effect of the blow was very exaggerated by the witness. 9. The book has been very improved by the revision. 10. While still at Oxford, he became very interested in social questions and for a number of years worked in the East End. 11. He is very interested in bird watching. 12. I wrote to General Parker about this and received a very nice letter from the General himself, saying he was very impressed with the material I had sent him. 13. Opera and theatre engagements are also very limited and by no means easy

Adverbs

to get. 14. I am very misunderstood. 15. And the King was very moved and went up to the chamber over the gate and wept. 16. He will be very pleased to edit the magazine. 17. The pictures were very praised by the critics. 18. In those days, towns were very separated from one another. 19. I was very surprised to see him. 20. She would have done it if she hadn't been so very tired. 21. I am very torn between the desire to go and the desire to stay. 22. The diet of marine species is generally very varied, and often changes considerably as the animals grow older and larger. 23. His wife was very worried too about Donald. 24. The enemy troops were very worried by frequent night attacks.

288 Insert *very* or *(very) much* as you think correct.

1. It was ..... like the bedrooms in seaside lodging houses. 2. He was no fool, and he was ..... interested in people. 3. I was ..... afraid of them. 4. Brown was a ..... travelled and well-informed man. 5. I was ..... impressed by the accuracy and fairness of your account. 6. His mind, ... occupied, received the picture from the eyes. 7. We are ..... limited in our powers. 8. She was dressed simply and neatly and she was ..... excited. 9. The herbaceous borders, planted with expensive seeds imported from Reading, are ..... envied in summer. 10. He's never been ..... concerned about politics. 11. I had felt ..... trapped the evening before and I seemed to have passed the night only half asleep. 12. He was a matter-of-fact man, not ..... given to emotion. 13. Mothers can be ..... distressed by fears that they may impulsively harm or kill their own babies. 14. The woman was ..... given to drink. 15. He knew well enough that he was not ..... beloved by anyone in that neighbourhood. 16. His tone was ..... annoyed. 17. The hotel manager was not ..... understanding either. 18. He was ..... in demand as a teacher. 19. He was ..... aware of what was going on although he didn't speak. 20. Johnnie and Elizabeth sound ..... alike when they talk. 21. Casement's treatment at Brixton Prison was ..... different from what he received in the Tower. 22. Even then, he was certain that motorcars would be ..... improved and brought within general use. 23. That was a ..... exciting play we saw last night. 24. The paintings were ..... admired by all the guests. 25. Your boss is ..... satisfied with you. 26. Granny gets ..... upset if people don't obey. 27. We ..... regret the mistake. 28. He lived snugly in Northamptonshire, ... respected by his neighbours. 29. He was ..... depressed at that time. 30. She recognized him, though his appearance was ..... changed. 31. The children were ..... disappointed to learn that there would be no picnic. 32. Bunting felt ..... put out.

Word Order

289 Rephrase the following sentences so that, for emphasis, the italicized expression comes at the beginning of the sentence.

1. The U.S. has *never before* been so tolerant of dissent. 2. In the three years of his service with the Captain he had *never* seen the room in such a state. 3. The former Soviet Premier has *rarely* been seen by the West, and he has *never* publicly discussed politics. 4. The managing editor heard the muttered interruptive commentary *only occasionally*. 5. Our hosts admitted *only once* that the overthrow of the old management had caused problems. 6. The firing had *no sooner* begun than Busty fell flat on his face with remarkable celerity. 7. Mr Davies *no sooner* got home than he had a very bad pain. 8. We had *hardly* arrived when I realized I had made a vast mistake. 9. Daisy had *scarcely* opened her lips when a loud ring and a knock echoed through the house. 10. They entertained at home *only* when they had a family party.

290 Sentences for translation.

1. Noch nie zuvor hatte er das Zimmer so ordentlich gesehen. 2. Und wenn ich hundert Jahre alt werde; niemals werde ich den fürchterlichen Geschmack dieser Flüssigkeit vergessen. 3. Selten wurde so vielen Protesten und Vorschlägen so wenig Beachtung geschenkt. 4. Nur gelegentlich schien er den Komfort eines warmen Bettes zu benötigen. 5. Nur dann können sie mit der freundschaftlichen Hilfe unseres Landes rechnen. 6. Erst jetzt wurde ihm klar, daß Bill und Mark schon immer enge Freunde gewesen waren. 7. Erst wenn die Situation schlimmer wird, wird unsere Gesellschaft besser werden. 8. Seit Juni 1965 hat kein amerikanischer Präsident oder Vizepräsident mehr den Kontinent besucht. 9. Seit den dreißiger Jahren ist kein amerikanischer Präsident mehr so groben Angriffen ausgesetzt gewesen wie Lyndon Johnson. 10. Unter keinen Umständen werden wir zulassen, daß ein ausländisches Schiff durch den Kanal fährt. 11. Nicht umsonst widmet er seine ganze Zeit dem Schreiben. 12. Weder in der Innenpolitik noch in der Außenpolitik hat er sich besonders hervorgetan. 13. Kaum hatten wir unsere Gläser hingestellt, da füllte der Kellner sie auch schon wieder nach. 14. Kaum habe ich das eine repariert, da geht das andere auch schon wieder kaputt. 15. Besonders fehlte den Browns die Oper. 16. Dann kam der Krieg. 17. Dann kam der Augenblick, wo der Angeklagte den Zeugenstand betrat. 18. Am nächsten Morgen kam ein Telegramm von Bill, aus dem hervorging, daß er am frühen Nachmittag ankommen würde. 19. Hinter ihm ging Herr Dr. Winter. 20. Auf dem Büfett waren Apfelsinen und Äpfel. 21. Von irgendwoher kam das Geräusch einer zuschlagenden Tür. 22. Die Tür ging auf, und herein spazierten die drei Missetäter. 23. Je mehr sie über sein Verhalten sprachen, desto seltsamer kam es ihnen vor.

291 Sentences for translation.

1. Wir wollen heute als unser Thema den Psalm 23 nehmen, den viele als die schönste Stelle in der Bibel ansehen. 2. Auf ein Ereignis kurz nach meiner Rück-

Word Order

kehr aus Schweden schaue ich mit großer Befriedigung zurück. 3. Weshalb willst du hier draußen wohnen? 4. Wozu brauchst du so viel Geld? 5. Der einzige, der mehr von der Landwirtschaft als David verstand, war Bennett. 6. Sie starteten ihre diplomatische Offensive unter anderem in der Absicht, ihre Gegenspieler weiter zu isolieren. 7. Er wußte über alles Bescheid, was in der Welt geschah, obwohl er blind war. 8. Im Grunde ist er kein allzu schlechter Kerl. 9. Im zweiten Stock wohnte Lorenheim. 10. Wozu wollen sie zu dieser Tageszeit eine kalte Dusche nehmen? 11. Dorothy sah plötzlich unglücklich aus. 12. Wie geht's? Fühlen Sie sich besser? 13. „Ich weiß nicht, was wir da machen können", sagte Jennifer schließlich. 14. Ich werde es dir später zurückgeben. 15. Wie kommt es, daß Sie noch hier sind?

292 Complete the following sentences by adding the objects in brackets.

1. It's a long document, and I'll give . . . . . after lunch. (it, you) 2. Why haven't you told . . . . . before? (this, anyone) 3. It was he who assigned . . . . . (this dirty work, me) 4. Why didn't they report . . . . .? (the incident, the police) 5. When I asked where the book came from, she said that the mother of the author had lent . . . . . (it, her) 6. Don't mention . . . . . (Jimmy Gordon, me) 7. Shall I recommend . . . . .? (a few books, you) 8. She forgot to take . . . . . (the hammer, Bill) 9. It's a long story, and I'll tell . . . . . later. (it, you) 10. This, in turn, had brought . . . . . (a mild prosperity, Adam) 11. She immediately telephoned . . . . . (the news, her husband) 12. But Luther does not offer . . . . . (any easy, adaptable solutions to Christian troubles, the Church).

293 Sentences for translation.

1. Sie goß ihm einen Whisky ein. 2. Die Pistole hatte Bill von seinem eigenen Vater geschenkt bekommen. 3. Sie las uns den Brief laut vor. 4. Pünktlich um halb acht brachte der Diener Sir Hugh seinen Orangensaft. 5. Können Sir mir ein gutes Wörterbuch empfehlen? 6. Bitte, belüg mich nicht! 7. Er fragte Charles nach seinem Namen. 8. Sie fragte, ob sie Zimmer frei hätten, und bemerkte, daß ihr das Haus von einem Freund empfohlen worden war. 9. Gib es ihr zurück! 10. Es schien unmöglich, daß ihn irgend jemand beneiden würde, weil er nach Paris fuhr. 11. Meine Mutter versprach uns ein Hochzeitsgeschenk. Sie sagte, sie würde es uns geben, wenn wir ein eigenes Haus bekämen. 12. Ich kann Ihnen nicht beschreiben, wie er aussah. 13. Er antwortete frei und offen, sogar auf Fragen, die man ihm nicht gestellt hatte. 14. Wo ist dein Pullover? Der, den ich dir gestrickt habe? 15. Ich habe Ihnen einen Vorschlag zu machen.

Prepositions

294 Supply prepositions where necessary.

1. Did you lose your foot ..... an accident? 2. I've got no money ..... my bank account at the moment. 3. He's got a thousand pounds ..... the savings bank. 4. She has a poet ..... a brother. 5. She couldn't sleep ..... excitement. 6. They wouldn't touch anything ..... fear ..... infection. 7. He had hurt his leg ..... a fall and was in the local hospital. 8. When Polar explorers find their food supplies running out, they often have to kill the sledge dogs ..... food. 9. They suffered badly ..... the hands of their captors. 10. The men of Pine Island said that ..... heart they wanted to be painters or writers or musicians. 11. Ben Nevis is the highest peak ..... the British Isles. 12. The car stopped suddenly ..... a red light. 13. I can dial the number ..... memory. 14. I once saw the ghost ..... a cold winter's night. 15. I wish my husband didn't have to work ..... nights. 16. We could hardly hear the priest ..... the noise of the guns and the wailing of silly, hysterical women. 17. Mary stayed in bed all day, ... the doctor's orders. 18. I'm out of bed now, but I'm still ..... doctor's orders. 19. Braddock won the fight ..... points. 20. He won fifteen hundred pounds ..... the football pools. 21. She was a librarian ..... profession.

295 Supply prepositions where necessary.

1. ..... the evenings I read or listen ..... concerts ..... the radio. 2. It is obvious that the gun was fired ..... close range. 3. He found the girl lying dead ..... the road. 4. He began to talk ..... greater speed. 5. Sailors and longshoremen unloaded passengers, cargo, and animals ..... great speed and dexterity. 6. Stephenson's famous "Rocket" pulled a load of seventeen tons ..... the then amazing speed of twenty-nine miles an hour. 7. A man named Spencer was detained by police ..... suspicion ..... being concerned ..... the Chapman murder. 8. In some urban areas, nearly half of all the residents stay ..... the streets at night ..... fear ..... attack. 9. He is ..... suspicion. 10. He said all this ..... a low voice. 11. "Rotten day, sir," I said, ... want of some other opening. 12. We're not ..... war with them yet. 13. They did not go out ..... fear of being seen. 14. She almost fainted ..... sheer joy. 15. The child fainted ..... hunger. 16. She was still pale ..... seasickness. 17. He joined the Navy ..... the name of Ronald Thornby. 18. George has been badly hurt ..... a motor-cycle accident. 19. He had a habit of muttering to himself ..... his breath. 20. I have an account ..... the Westminster Bank. 21. I noticed that there was whisky ..... his breath. 22. The slanders of his political opponents are ..... contempt. 23. Sarah Bernhardt didn't believe motion pictures ..... the dignity of her art. 24. It's only fifteen miles ..... foot. It'd be fifty ..... road. 25. They travelled back to London ..... the 8.04 train. 26. They have a house ..... Long Island. 27. Many different kinds of meat are sold ..... the market.

Prepositions

296 Supply prepositions where necessary.

1. I read the book from cover to cover ..... one weekend. 2. Dogson is a reporter ..... the local evening paper. 3. He used to play football ..... the high-school team. 4. Do you recognize the lady ..... the photograph? 5. There were swans swimming ..... the pond. 6. They're hoping to win a fortune ..... the pools. 7. It isn't good to drink whisky ..... an empty stomach. 8. They were arrested ..... suspicion of having been concerned ..... the plot to assassinate the dictator. 9. If you don't quit ..... your own accord, I'll fire you. 10. I'm doing this ..... my own free will. 11. He failed to see the wood ..... the trees. 12. They met ..... Lyons, and had a cup of tea. 13. I couldn't sleep ..... night ..... the noise. 14. What do you do ..... relaxation? 15. Once again, the little hand is ..... the six, the big hand is ..... the twelve, and it's time for the Six O'Clock Report. 16. What does a woman like you have to cry about ..... a morning like this? 17. His eyes gleamed ..... excitement. 18. Her face glowed ..... indignation. 19. The patient screamed ..... pain.

297 Supply prepositions where necessary.

1. She cherished a profound devotion ..... him and probably dreamed ..... him at night. 2. It is difficult to find an explanation ..... her conduct. 3. Surely you must have great influence ..... the boss. 4. His genuine warmth and love ..... people made him well-liked ..... everyone. 5. They will have no mercy ..... him. 6. Ken found his fists doubling up ..... the very thought of the name ..... Hunter. 7. There's a teacher there ..... the name ..... Miss Wriggly. 8. The next morning he took a plane ..... Ann Arbor. 9. Her pleasure ..... seeing me seemed unfeigned. 10. She took great pride ..... her achievements. 11. His relief ..... being out of harm's way was immense. 12. There is no visible solution ..... the problem as it is today. 13. They're on a visit ..... Europe. 14. She waited, longingly, for his return ..... home. 15. He's a genius ..... repairing broken hearts. 16. Her marriage ..... him was dissolved. 17. He had an aversion ..... easy promises and theatricalized results. 18. He gave him a cheque ..... two hundred and fifty pounds. 19. The town ..... Briarwood was unusually quiet. 20. He was a witness ..... the crime.

298 Supply prepositions where necessary.

1. He wasn't very able ..... deception and love affairs. 2. The rum was almost black ..... colour, and smelt ..... treacle. 3. His black eyes were bright ..... triumph. 4. Her eldest brother is clever ..... making things. 5. We got quite expert ..... getting the worms out. 6. He was glad ..... a chance to escape. 7. Map-reading is a thing Peter is really good ..... 8. For some time she had been ill ..... heart failure. 9. Really, the police are sometimes expected to solve

Prepositions

problems incapable ..... solution. 10. He was jealous ..... the publicity I was getting. 11. In England everybody is keen ..... birds and their habits. 12. The coat is a little short ..... the sleeves. 13. She was shy ..... strangers. 14. The child had taken sick ..... an inflammation of the lungs. 15. She looked quite surprised ..... seeing me. 16. People here are deeply suspicious ..... any newcomer. 17. He's very useful ..... the house. 18. Welcome ..... home ..... God's country! 19. The boats were still wet ..... rain. 20. She was white ..... anger. 21. It was uncomfortable standing there in the cold, covered ..... nothing but wet soap.

299 Supply prepositions where necessary.

1. The book was torn, tattered and dog-eared ..... use. 2. He was naturally elated ..... the knowledge of his imminent return to England. 3. I am not impressed ..... what he has written. 4. Chris was impressed ..... what he saw. 5. She is married ..... a nuclear physicist. 6. He was no more than a cold-hearted vulgarian, much preoccupied ..... money and women, but possessed ..... neither. 7. He was grief-stricken ..... the death of his pet. 8. He was struck ..... her ability as a teacher. 9. Those beloved ..... the Gods die young. 10. I've been frightened ..... ghosts all my life. 11. He isn't good ..... making money. 12. Ted Farlough was good ..... the trumpet, and Fred Cohn was terrific ..... the drums. 13. He was very angry ..... the delay. 14. He seemed glad ..... my company. 15. I was glad ..... this opportunity to see her again. 16. I think he's jealous ..... the attention I'm getting. 17. It's close ..... six o'clock and Jim will be back soon. 18. The children believed that the whole bottom of the lake was covered ..... gold. 19. The old woman's skin was remarkably free ..... wrinkles.

300 Supply prepositions where necessary.

1. He is blind ..... his left eye. 2. He is slightly crippled ..... one arm. 3. He has been lame ..... his left leg since childhood. 4. She had been ill ..... nephritis and a heart disease. 5. At the age of six or seven he had fallen seriously ill ..... mumps. 6. Of all the cities he had visited, he was most vividly impressed ..... San Francisco. 7. Professor Hinton is married ..... two children. 8. He is married ..... a very rich woman. 9. You are new ..... this city? 10. Indonesia is rich ..... natural resources. 11. He became obsessed ..... the thought of early death. 12. She was so overcome ..... horror that she locked herself in her room and began to cry. 13. He was weak ..... fear. 14. He was wet ..... sweat.

301 Supply prepositions where necessary.

1. They readily agreed ..... my suggestion. 2. His story of the collision agrees ..... mine. 3. I agree ..... you ..... that point. 4. He plans to appeal .....

Prepositions

his sentence. 5. She arrived ..... home breathless. 6. He asked me ..... my opinion ..... the club. 7. He asked him ..... the woman's name. 8. He asked him ..... some water. 9. This was the first time she ever asked an important question ..... her daughter. 10. May I ask you how you came ..... the manuscript? 11. I breakfasted ..... fresh figs, which I had never eaten before. 12. I don't care much ..... food. 13. Come ..... the kitchen if you don't mind the squalor. 14. Nothing came ..... this idea. 15. Were you dreaming ..... Polly Newton? 16. They certainly envied me ..... my unearned money. 17. What do you think of these silent people, my mind asked hers; do you envy them ..... being at home in this comfortable country, so settled and cosy and safe? 18. What sustained them was the belief that they were fighting ..... a good cause. 19. Would you like to go ..... the waiting room? 20. I shouldn't grudge them ..... their little hour of health and strength.

302 Supply prepositions where necessary.

1. You could get the same effect ..... jumping ..... the river ..... a cold night. 2. She hung up ..... me. 3. Would you like to join us ..... lunch? 4. Would you like to join us ..... a cup of tea? 5. Other people would jump ..... an offer like this. 6. The old man was well known ..... an incurable invader. 7. She lamented ..... the misery she had brought ..... her family. 8. They lived ..... diets that either were low ..... fat, or substituted polyunsaturated fats ..... saturated fats wherever possible. 9. You look ..... an honest man. 10. He was pacing ..... his office furiously. 11. I refused to play ..... cowboys and Indians with the other children. 12. I don't like military parades and people who play ..... soldiers. 13. They're playing ..... detectives. 14. In those days, kings and princes played ..... war the way Englishmen play ..... hunting. 15. He means well ..... you. 16. I practised a lot ..... paddling a canoe and rowing. 17. I always set my watch ..... the clock in the library. 18. What are you smiling ..... ? 19. He spends a great deal ..... clothes. 20. Do you still stand ..... your statement that you don't think he's the boy who smashed the window? 21. This ice cream tastes ..... soap.

303 Supply prepositions where necessary.

1. What were you thinking ..... ? 2. Some people thrive ..... flattery. 3. I took ..... him at first sight and we became firm friends. 4. If there's anything you want ..... me, just call ..... me. 5. I went ..... the back door of my bungalow and directly into my office. 6. He drove two blocks past the house, parked, returned ..... foot, and walked ..... the front door. 7. As I watched, a tall figure came ..... a side door. 8. He went ..... the door without another word. 9. He insured his wife's life ..... five hundred pounds. 10. Will you join me ..... a cup of tea? 11. He is something of a charmer and has lived ..... his wits all his life. 12. They don't hurt drunks in Las Vegas – they live .....

Prepositions

them. 13. I look ..... the bright side of things. 14. I felt that fate meant well ..... me. 15. I made up my mind this afternoon ..... what I'm going to do. 16. The old man nodded ..... his white head. 17. At the hospital, she was immediately operated ..... 18. He paid ..... the meal ..... cheque. 19. He was defeated ..... points. 20. He practises ..... the piano two hours a day.

Supply prepositions where necessary. **304**

1. I'm prepared to resign ..... my job. 2. I always set my watch ..... the time signal ..... the radio. 3. He set the alarm ..... seven o'clock. 4. Our son doesn't set much store ..... chocolate. 5. No other professor in Great Britain sets such store ..... being called Professor. 6. The teacher sets a high value ..... neatness. 7. He used to spend all his pocket money ..... naughty books. 8. Sherlock Holmes told Watson that the most villainous-looking man of his acquaintance was a philanthropist who had spent half a million ..... the London poor, while the most charming woman he had ever seen poisoned her husband and three children ..... their insurance money. 9. From the moment of their first meeting they talked ..... escape. 10. Must you men always talk ..... business? 11. In the evening he paid a visit ..... the village inn. 12. Mother and I have been waiting ..... supper for you. 13. I tried to figure out what these people could possibly want ..... me. 14. This is a fate I would not wish ..... my worst enemy. 15. The man had died ..... prolonged starvation and neglect. 16. Bill's father had recently died ..... shrapnel wounds suffered in the war. 17. What did the cat die ..... ? 18. His stomach hurt ..... hunger. 19. He collapsed ..... thirst and exhaustion.

Supply prepositions where necessary. **305**

1. They told her that he had admitted ..... the murder of her husband. 2. Shortly after he was arrested, the man confessed ..... the crime. 3. They arrived ..... home at noon. 4. All asked ..... his health. 5. People didn't ask much ..... life in those days. 6. I have never asked a favour ..... you in my life. 7. He then inquired ..... the lawyer's fee. 8. He inquired ..... the landlord the price of a room. 9. A noisy woman who had lost her handbag was loudly blaming her husband ..... his carelessness. 10. He met Jack outside ..... a café in Ladbroke Grove and bought a suitcase ..... him. 11. Colchester Academy was a good school which catered not only ..... the children of the divorced, the widowed, and the sick, but ..... those with intellectual or social ambitions unattainable at home. 12. She closed the door ..... us. 13. That's what comes ..... being a total abstainer. 14. He complimented Senator Dodd ..... being such a persistent interrogator. 15. They congratulated him ..... his marriage. 16. The widow's friends condoled ..... her at the funeral. 17. I don't think they'll declare war ..... the United States. 18. Clifford departed ..... the White House in 1950. 19. Next morning she was up at seven, donned

Prepositions

a tan cardigan, skirt and brown blouse and breakfasted heartily ..... bacon and eggs. 20. We lunched ..... poached eggs on toast, cake, and tea.

306 Supply prepositions where necessary.

1. He dined not too badly ..... local-caught fish and stewed fruit. 2. I got drunk ..... rum last night. 3. We drank ..... Bob's health. 4. I don't think that he died ..... his own hand. 5. The doctors agreed that the man had not died ..... natural causes. 6. Each year, almost 150 U.S. children die ..... aspirin poisoning. 7. He died ..... a heart attack. 8. He was satisfied that Mrs Finch had not died ..... suffocation by smoke. 9. He died this morning in the hospital ..... pneumonia. 10. He enclosed a cheque ..... the letter. 11. I envy you ..... your excellent health. 12. I don't grudge the girl ..... her bit of pleasure. 13. Pearson was born in Newburyport on February 11, 1880, ... a long-established family. 14. The girl fled ..... the room. 15. This publishing firm specializes ..... language textbooks. 16. Nowadays scholars tend to specialize ..... one particular branch of a subject.

307 Sentences for translation.

an 1. Was würdest du tun, wenn du an meiner Stelle wärest? 2. Köln liegt am Rhein. 3. Es sind ein paar hübsche Bilder an der Wand. 4. Als ich ihn das letzte Mal sah, ging er immer noch an Krücken. 5. Hunde sind an der Leine zu führen. 6. Soll ich sie an der Hand führen? 7. An seinen Behauptungen ist nichts Wahres. 8. Ist das alles, was Sie an Gepäck haben? 9. Er ist an Krebs gestorben. 10. Viele starben an Unterernährung. 11. Sie ergötzte sich an meiner Verwirrung. 12. Er kam am Abend an. 13. Er kam am Abend des 13. Oktober an. 14. Ich kann Sie nicht an der Teilnahme hindern. 15. Zu meinem Entsetzen nahm seine Stimme jetzt einen drohenden Ton an.

auf 1. Der Ben Nevis ist der höchste Berg auf den Britischen Inseln. 2. Auf diesem Bild ist er nicht mit dabei. 3. Seit dem Unfall ist er auf einem Ohr taub. 4. Warum setzt du dich nicht auf diesen Stuhl? 5. Es geht auf Mitternacht zu. 6. Im Englischen gibt es Hunderte von Substantiven, die auf -y enden. 7. Wir hatten ein Zimmer mit Blick auf die Berge. 8. Der ist nur auf ihr Geld aus! 9. Ich freue mich auf unser Wiedersehen in Leeds. 10. So etwas kann man doch nicht auf ein bloßes Gerücht hin tun! 11. Er schwört auf seinen Zahnarzt. 12. Auf Ihr Wohl!

aus 1. Man kann eine Sprache nicht ausschließlich aus Büchern lernen. 2. Wir kommen gerade aus Glasgow. 3. Dieses Hemd ist aus einem neuartigen Kunststoff. 4. Nach dem Kriege machte man Kochtöpfe aus Soldatenhelmen. 5. Er macht sich nicht viel aus Musik. 6. Aus dem Jungen werden wir nie einen Gelehrten machen können. 7. Er nahm sich aus Verzweiflung das Leben. 8. Die

Prepositions

Pflanzen sind aus Mangel an Wasser eingegangen. 9. Er ist aus freien Stücken zu uns gekommen.

bei 1. Er wohnt bei seiner Mutter. 2. Das hast du doch nicht bei Woolworth gekauft! 3. Ich habe ihn bei Hertie getroffen. 4. Wir haben mehrere Konten bei der Midland Bank. 5. Viele seiner Kunden arbeiten bei Ford. 6. Er ist Reporter beim Daily Express. 7. Hast du die Zeitung bei dir? 8. Hast du das Geld bei dir? 9. So was kann man doch nicht bei Kerzenlicht machen! 10. Kannst du die Schlüssel nicht beim Hausmeister lassen? 11. Laß uns das doch bei einem Glas Bier besprechen!

bis 1. Ich kann Sie bis Nottingham mitnehmen. 2. Er folgte mir bis ins Zimmer. 3. Er hat bis jetzt noch nicht ein einziges Spiel gewonnen. 4. Hat er nicht bis vor einem Jahr in Berlin gewohnt? 5. Das Museum bleibt bis auf weiteres geschlossen. 6. Ich muß bis sechs wieder zurück sein.

durch 1. Er wurde durch einen verläßlicheren Mann ersetzt. 2. Ich habe davon durch die Zeitung erfahren. 3. Das wird durch die Spritze besser werden.

für 1. Diese Art von Einstellung ist typisch für ihn. 2. Er ist so was wie ein Experte für Seevögel. 3. Mehrere seiner ehemaligen Patienten haben für ihn ausgesagt. 4. Ein Beispiel für diese Einstellung findet sich in den Werken von Virginia Woolf. 5. Es ließ sich kein Beweis für seine Schuld finden.

in 1. Er hat in Edinburgh studiert. 2. Er hat in Edinburgh gewohnt. 3. Der Arzt kam noch in der Nacht. 4. Wir werden in den nächsten Wochen viel zu tun haben. 5. Ich habe in den letzten Tagen mehrfach versucht, dich anzurufen. 6. Ich habe es im Radio gehört. 7. Ist er schon mal im Fernsehen aufgetreten? 8. Er kommt heute in vierzehn Tagen. 9. In einer Stunde bin ich bei dir.

mit 1. Er schreibt alle seine Briefe mit dem Bleistift. 2. Er mußte das gerade erworbene Bild mit Verlust verkaufen. 3. Er tötete fünf Fliegen mit einem einzigen Schlag. 4. Er fuhr mit einer Geschwindigkeit von 80 Stundenkilometern, als es zu dem Unfall kam. 5. „Ich würde ihn nicht gerade schüchtern nennen", sagte sie mit leiser Stimme. 6. Er übersah die Situation mit einem Blick.

nach 1. Er fragte mich nach dem Preis. 2. Sie wurde nach ihrem Namen gefragt. 3. Er hat sich nach dir erkundigt. 4. Die Suppe schmeckt furchtbar nach Knoblauch. 5. Wann ist er nach London abgefahren?

über 1. Ich war über diese Nachricht nicht überrascht. 2. Ich war über ihren Mangel an Verständnis enttäuscht. 3. Ich war sehr über ihn enttäuscht. 4. Er hat die Unverschämtheit besessen, mir eine Rechnung über fünfzehn Pfund zu schicken. 5. Warum fahren Sie nicht über Harwich? 6. Laß uns nicht über Politik reden!

Prepositions

um   1. Niemand beneidet sie um diesen Mann.   2. Er bat mich um einen Gefallen.   3. Er bat mich um Hilfe.   4. Hast du den Wagen denn nicht um die Ecke kommen sehen?

von   1. Was wollten die von uns?   2. Das Kind fiel vom Stuhl.   3. Unsere Straße geht von der Hauptstraße ab.   4. Die Menschen hier leben hauptsächlich von Reis.   5. Er lebt vom Bücherschreiben.

vor   1. Er konnte vor Angst nicht sprechen.   2. Die Kinder konnten vor Aufregung nicht schlafen.   3. Er war außer sich vor Freude.   4. Sie waren vor Furcht geradezu gelähmt.   5. Er starb vor Hunger.   6. Da ist jemand vor der Tür.

zu   1. Er wurde zum König gekrönt.   2. Wird er seine Versprechungen halten, wenn man ihn zum Präsidenten wählt?   3. Er wurde zum Hauptmann befördert.   4. Man hat ihn zum Ehrenvorsitzenden ernannt.   5. Sie kamen sehr spät zu Hause an.   6. Es gab Brathuhn zu Mittag.   7. Meist geht's zum einen Ohr 'rein und zum anderen wieder 'raus.   8. Man hat mir dieses Buch zur Ansicht geschickt.

Index

The numbers refer to sections, not to pages.

a(n) 247–257
abhor 5
able 161
absolute *-ing* construction 68–69
accusative of (pro)noun 64–65
accusative with infinitive 32–45
accustomed 14
A.c.I. 32–45
acknowledge 35
active vs. passive infinitive 24–27
adjective into noun 276–277
adjectives: comparison 272–275
admit 14, 35
adore 4, 6
adverbs 278–288
advise 35–36
affect 5
afford 5
afraid 15
agreement 225–234
allow 35, 37
alternative 11
anomalous finites 151–207
anxious 12
any vs. *some* 268–269
arrange 7
articles 237–257
ashamed 12
ask 36
attempt 9
auxiliaries 151–207
averse 13

bear 4, 34, 67
beg 35, 36
begin 3, 7
believe 33
be past 67
be to 177–178, 190–191
be worth 67
bid 35
blame 24, 27
bother 4–5
BRAUCHEN 198
burst out 6
busy 70

can 158, 169–170
capable 12
case problems 64–65, 267
catenatives 3–8, 14
cause 33, 35
cease 4, 6
certify 35
challenge 34
chance 9–11
chary 12
choose 6
command 35–36
commence 5
committed 13
comparison of adjectives 272–275
compel 35
concord 225–234
conditional sentences 142–147
confess 14
consent 14
consider 7–8, 33
contemplate 8
continue 5
continuous form: see progressive form
contrive 4–5
could 159–161, 169
courage 10

dare 34, 36, 156–157
dead-set 12
debate 5
decide 4, 36
declare 35
decline 7
defective auxiliaries 151–207
definite article 237–246
defy 34, 36
deny 6, 37
deserve 67
desire 33
destined 13
determination 9
determine 32
detest 4
devote 14
difficulty 11

149

direct object: position 292–293
discontinue 5
disdain 4
dislike 35
disposed 13
doubt 126
dread 6
drive 35
durative form: see progressive form
DÜRFEN 193

embarrassed 12
emphasizing pronouns 258–259
enable 35
encourage 32
endeavour 7
enjoy 4, 6
entitled 13
entreat 35
ES 271
expanded form: see progressive form
expect 33, 35

feel 33, 35–37
feel like 70
finish 5
forbid 36
forget 7
for + infinitive group 46–50
fortunate 13
future 125–141

gender 235–236
genitive 64–65, 219–221
gerund: see *-ing* form
get 14
get around 14
given 13
give sb. to understand 36
going to 125, 129–130, 133–135, 147
got 151–155
guess 37
guilty 13

habit 9–10
hate 3–6, 37
have 34–37
have (got) 151–155
have to 190–191
hear 32, 37
help 8, 35
hesitate 6
hesitation 10
hold 33
honour 10
hope 9, 126

if clauses 142–147
implore 35
impulse 11
inclination 11
indefinite article 247–257
indirect object: position 292–293
indirect speech 148–150
induce 32, 35
infinitive 1, 3–15, 17–56
infinitive: active or passive? 24–27
infinitive after interrogatives 17–18
infinitive equivalent to adverbial clause 21–23
infinitive equivalent to relative clause 19–20, 266
infinitive group 32–45
infinitive group preceded by *for* 46–50
infinitive or *-ing* form? 3–15
infinitive preceded by *with(out)* + (pro)noun 51–52
infinitive: present vs. perfect 53–56
infinitive: syntactic functions 1
-ing construction: absolute 68–69
-ing construction equivalent to subordinate clause 57–62
-ing form 2, 3–16, 57–74
-ing form: idiomatic uses 16
-ing form: misrelated 63
-ing form or infinitive? 3–15
-ing form preceded by (pro)noun 64–66
-ing form: syntactic functions 2
-ing form with passive meaning 67
instinct 10
instruct 32
intend 33, 37
intention 9, 11
interested 12
interrogatives 262–263
interrogatives + infinitive 17–18
inversion 289–290
invite 35
irregular verbs 210–211
it 270
it's no good 4

keen 12
keep 8
keep on 8
knack 11
know 33–34
KÖNNEN 192

lead 32
learn 3, 6
leave 32
let 36

liable 13
like 5, 7–8, 33, 36–37
linking verbs 278, 283
live 119
loath 13
look forward 14
loss 11
love 6
-ly ending 278–288

make 36–37
may 162, 165, 169–171, 208
mean 3–5, 8, 34
means 10
might 166–169, 171
misfortune 11
misrelated *-ing* form 63
miss 44
modal auxiliaries 151–207
much vs. *very* 287–288
MÜSSEN 196
must 189–191

need 67, 156–157, 190–191
neglect 6
notice 35–37
noun + *-ing* form 64–66
number form of nouns 222–224

object form of (pro)noun 64–65
object + infinitive 32–45
objection 9
objects: position 292–293
observe 33, 36
occasion 10
omit 6
one: prop word 276–277
opportunity 9–11
oppose 7
order 35
ought to 188, 190
overhear 36–37

participle: see *-ing* form
particles 294–307
passive 212–218
passive infinitive 24–27
passive meaning of *-ing* form 67
past 67
past perfect 123–124
past simple 93–95
past simple vs. progressive 96–98
past vs. present perfect 107–113
perceive 36
perfect infinitive 53–56

persuade 32
plan 5
plural form of nouns 222–223
plural or singular? 222–223, 225–234
point 11
possessive adjectives 260–261
possessive form 64–65, 219–220
postpone 8
practise 6
precaution 11
prefer 3, 5, 33, 36
prepositions 294–307
present participle: see *-ing* form
present perfect: miscellaneous exercises 122
present perfect simple vs. progressive 114–118
present perfect vs. past 107–113
present simple 75–76, 125–126, 129, 135
present simple vs. progressive 77–92
present vs. perfect infinitive 53–56
progressive form to express futurity 125, 129–130, 135
progressive vs. simple form 99–106
progressive vs. simple form of *live* 119
progressive vs. simple past 96–98
progressive vs. simple present 77–92
progressive vs. simple present perfect 114–118
pro-infinitive 28–29
prompt 36
prone 13
pronoun + *-ing* 64–66
propose 3–4
prop word *one* 276–277
proud 12
punctuation 264

question tags 185, 200–203
quit 7

recommend 35–36
reflexive pronouns 258–259
regret 5
relative clause replaced by infinitive 19–20, 266
relative clause replaced by *-ing* construction 59
relative clauses 264–266
relative pronouns 264–266
relish 7
remember 3–6
report 36
reported speech 148–150
reputation 10
request 35–36
require 33, 35–36, 67
resent 6
resist 5–6

right 9–10
risk 7

see 14, 32, 36–37
see fit 7
-self pronouns 258–259
set about 4
-'s form of noun 64–65, 219–220
shall 127, 175–177, 179
short responses 204–207
should 180–183, 190, 208
signal 35
simple past 93–95
simple present 75–76, 125, 129, 135
simple vs. progressive form 99–106
simple vs. progressive form of *live* 119
simple vs. progressive past 96–98
simple vs. progressive present 77–92
simple vs. progressive present perfect 114–118
since 120–121
SOLLEN 195
some vs. *any* 268–269
split infinitive 30–31
start 7
state 36
stoop 14
stop 3–5, 7
subjunctive 208–209
subordinate clause replaced by *-ing* construction 57–62
substantivization of adjectives 276–277
suffer 33
suggest 6
suppose 33, 36
surprise 9

tag questions 185, 200–203
tail questions 185, 200–203
take 14

tell 33, 36
tempt 34
temptation 10
tenses 75–150
testify 14
thank 34
the 237–246
think 37
trust 33–34
try 3–4, 7–8

unaccustomed 14
urge 11, 32
used to 184–187

value 6
very vs. *much* 287–288
view 11
volunteer 8

want 33, 36–37, 67
watch 33, 36–37
way 10–11
WERDEN 197
will 172, 179
willingness 9
will/shall 125–126, 128, 130, 134–135
will/shall + *going to* 125
will/shall + *-ing* 125, 130, 135–138
wish 11, 35–36
with(out) + (pro)noun + infinitive 51–52
WOLLEN 194
wont 13
word order 286, 289–293
worth 67, 70
would 173–174, 183, 186–187

yearn 7